Microfinance

Palgrave Macmillan Studies in Banking and Financial Institutions

Series Editor: **Professor Philip Molyneux**

The Palgrave Macmillan Studies in Banking and Financial Institutions will be international in orientation and include studies of banking within particular countries or regions, and studies of particular themes such as Corporate Banking, Risk Management, Mergers and Acquisitions, etc. The books will be focused upon research and practice, and include up-to-date and innovative studies on contemporary topics in banking that will have global impact and influence.

Titles include:

Yener Altunbas, Blaise Gadanecz and Alper Kara
SYNDICATED LOANS
A Hybrid of Relationship Lending and Publicly Traded Debt

Santiago Carbó, Edward P.M. Gardener and Philip Molyneux
FINANCIAL EXCLUSION

Franco Fiordelisi and Philip Molyneux
SHAREHOLDER VALUE IN BANKING

Munawar Iqbal and Philip Molyneux
THIRTY YEARS OF ISLAMIC BANKING
History, Performance and Prospects

Mario La Torre and Gianfranco A. Vento
MICROFINANCE

Philip Molyneux and Munawar Iqbal
BANKING AND FINANCIAL SYSTEMS IN THE ARAB WORLD

Andrea Schertler
THE VENTURE CAPITAL INDUSTRY IN EUROPE

Alfred Slager
THE INTERNATIONALIZATION OF BANKS
Patterns, Strategies and Performance

Palgrave Macmillan Studies in Banking and Financial Institutions
Series Standing Order ISBN 1–4039–4872–0

You can receive future titles in this series as they are published by placing a standing order. Please contact your bookseller or, in case of difficulty, write to us at the address below with your name and address, the title of the series and one of the ISBNs quoted above.

Customer Services Department, Macmillan Distribution Ltd, Houndmills, Basingstoke, Hampshire RG21 6XS, England

---

Microfinance

Mario La Torre

and

Gianfranco A. Vento

With contributions from Monica M. Ortolani, Silvia Trezza and Marco Tutino

First published in 2006 by
PALGRAVE MACMILLAN
Houndmills, Basingstoke, Hampshire RG21 6XS and
175 Fifth Avenue, New York, N.Y. 10010
Companies and representatives throughout the world

PALGRAVE MACMILLAN is the global academic imprint of the Palgrave
Macmillan division of St. Martin's Press, LLC and of Palgrave Macmillan Ltd.
Macmillan® is a registered trademark in the United States, United Kingdom
and other countries. Palgrave is a registered trademark in the European
Union and other countries.

ISBN-13: 978–1–4039–9789–0 hardback
ISBN-10: 1–4039–9789–6 hardback

This book is printed on paper suitable for recycling and made from fully
managed and sustained forest sources.

A catalogue record for this book is available from the British Library.

Library of Congress Cataloging-in-Publication Data

La Torre, Mario.
    Microfinance / Mario La Torre and Gianfranco A. Vento; with
contributions from Monica Ortolani, Silvia Trezza, and Marco Tutino.
        p. cm.—(Palgrave Macmillan studies in banking and financial
    institutions)
    Includes bibliographical references and index.
    ISBN 1–4039–9789–6 (cloth)
        1. Microfinance. I. Vento, Gianfranco A., 1975– II. Title. III. Series.

HG178.3.L3 2006
332—dc22   2006043257

10 9 8 7 6 5 4 3 2 1
15 14 13 12 11 10 09 08 07 06

Printed and bound in Great Britain by
Antony Rowe Ltd, Chippenham and Eastbourne

Immo non perditurus: eo loco sit donatio undi repeti non debeat,
reddi posit. (*Seneca*, De vita beata, *xxiv, 2*)

Contents

List of Tables

List of Figures

List of Boxes

Preface and Acknowledgements

This book presents a current analysis of the financial aspects of microfinance. It is unique in that it utilizes a banking risk-management approach to address the financial management of microfinance institutions and projects. This work has been possible owing to the specific expertise of each of the authors. The book is the result of contributions from different researchers from the Microfinance Research Group of the Banking Department of the University of Rome 'La Sapienza', coordinated by Professor Mario La Torre. The Group has a long history of collaboration with many Italian NGOs that promote microfinance programmes around the world. Moreover, the Group has been heavily involved in the activities of the Italian National Committee for '2005: the International Year of Microcredit' – proclaimed by the United Nations – and adopted by the Italian Ministry of Foreign Affairs.

For this book, Professor La Torre has coordinated the contributions of a team of four researchers specialized in banking and financial management (Monica Ortolani, Silvia Trezza, and Gianfranco Vento – University of Rome 'La Sapienza' – and Marco Tutino – University of Rome III), which collectively has significant experience in microfinance.

The operational experience in microfinance, combined with the theoretical and managerial expertise in the banking field has allowed the authors to develop a microfinance handbook which approaches microfinance financial management with the same instruments adopted by traditional banks, without compromising the particular nature of microfinance. We believe that this effort will assist microfinance management while offering support to microfinance practitioners in developing financial strategies with a scientific approach, without complicating the practice of microfinance itself.

We would like to thank the members of the Italian National Committee for '2005: the International Year of Microcredit'.

Finally, thanks to Nicola Allan, Jami Hubbard and Tommaso Caselli, our English proof-readers.

MARIO LA TORRE
GIANFRANCO A. VENTO

Notes on the Contributors

Mario La Torre is Full Professor in Banking and Finance and Director of the MA course in Film Art Management at the University of Rome 'La Sapienza'. His main area of research is on the financial management and financial innovation of the banking and financial services industry and he has published widely in this area. Main texts include: *Securitisation and Banks*; *Postbank in Italy*; and *Mergers & Acquisitions in Banking*. Recent articles concern microfinance: 'Modern microfinance: the role of banks'; 'Ethical Finance and Microfinance'. Professor La Torre has acted as a consultant to various banks, public institutions and consulting firms. He has directed the Research Group of the Italian National Committee for '2005: International Year of Microcredit'. He is on the Scientific Board of various NGOs and Financial Institutions operating in the microfinance sector.

Monica M. Ortolani is currently a PhD student in Banking and Finance at University of Rome 'La Sapienza'. She has been a member of different research groups for the Italian National Committee for '2005: International Year of Microcredit'. After working in Total Quality Management for a banking consulting company, she is now working in internal control systems for a banking consultant. Her current research includes: microfinance; banks' internal control systems and risk management; she is the author of several articles in top academic journals.

Silvia Trezza is currently a PhD student with grant research in Banking and Finance at the University of Rome 'La Sapienza'. She has been a member of different research groups for the Italian National Committee for the '2005: International Year of Microcredit'. Current research includes, microfinance, credit risk management and credit risk mitigation.

Marco Tutino (MA, PhD) is currently lecturer in Business Administration at the University of Rome III. He has been a member of different research groups of the Italian National Committee for '2005: International Year of Microcredit'. His main research interest relates to corporate strategy, performance measurement, business evaluation and finance. His research has been published by Italian academic journals.

Gianfranco A. Vento (MSc, PhD) is post-doctoral scholar in Microfinance at the University of Rome 'La Sapienza'. He has been member of different research groups for the Italian National Committee for

'2005: International Year of Microcredit'. He has followed several microfinance projects in developing countries for an Italian NGO. He used to be an analyst in the Banking Supervision Department at the Bank of Italy. His main research interest relates to the money market and microfinance. His research has been published by leading Italian academic journals. He is the author of *Interbank Market and Eurosystem*.

Introduction

Mario La Torre

This book is not a macroeconomic study for policy-makers; it is not a survey of best practices in microfinance; it is not a guide for practitioners and donors. Instead, it is a tool for individuals interested in analysing microfinance using a banking managerial approach modified for the specificities of microfinance.

Microfinance literature has been characterized by different trends over the past decades. In the early 1980s, microcredit and microfinance arose as alternatives to traditional development policies. Economists and policy-makers have tried to examine, both in theory and in practice, the impact of microfinance on socioeconomic policies for developing countries. This has inspired a great number of studies, mainly focused on the macroeconomic effects of microfinance and impact studies dedicated to different countries, sectors or types of beneficiaries. For years the macroeconomic approach has been basically the only view-point presented in microfinance literature. During those early years, the need to explore and to diffuse knowledge and information about microfinance globally has resulted in a focus on the most significant experiences. There have been countless publications detailing success stories from various countries and promoted by different institutions which have been and which remain in fashion. Further, the diffusion of these success stories as examples or models for future programmes has encouraged a new trend of *best practice literature*.

From the very beginning, microcredit and microfinance have been studied mostly from a macroeconomic and operational point of view. This book, however, follows a different trajectory – microeconomic from the managerial perspective. Modern microfinance has expanded its functions compared with the very first *microcredit* experiences. New trends have dramatically altered microfinance features, in terms of beneficiaries, products and the institutions involved. Microfinance is no longer just a financial technique principally offered by the non-profit sector as part of development programmes to sustain the poor in developing countries. It has become something more. The modern microfinance market is characterized by a complex demand for financial

and technical services, and a complex supply, owing to a growing inter-action and interest on the part of institutional donors, the non-profit sector and the financial markets.

Fluctuations in microfinance supply and demand have shifted the attention of researchers and practitioners towards alternative and inno-vative management tools for microfinance. This trend has given birth to a new series of studies, principally focused on the performance of micro-finance programmes and microfinance institutions (MFIs). In turn, this has spurred the creation of microeconomic literature for microfinance. The microeconomic approach analyses, mostly, the trade-off between financial performance and the ethical goals implicit in every microfi-nance initiative. From this perspective, specific accountancy rules and standards have been implemented and different models for financial performance analysis have been evolved.

This book goes one step further: it takes microfinance into the field of risk management. Therefore, the main objective of this text is to extend the risk management approach used by traditional banks to encompass microfinance as well. This kind of analysis simultaneously offers a great advantage and carries a great risk: on the one hand, it can help MFIs to attain higher levels of efficiency. On the other hand, it can cause a drift from the original spirit of microfinance, which is based on having a flex-ible organizational structure, easy procedures and informal relationships.

For these reasons the authors of this book have put substantial effort into analysing the fundamentals of banking management, which could also apply to microfinance, and which could be particularly useful to microfinance practitioners who aim to collaborate with banks and financial intermediaries, as well as to informal and formal MFIs. We have thus adopted the standard risk management approach utilized by banks, adapting it accordingly to the exigencies of the microfinance process. The main aspects of risk management have been considered, with the exclusion of risk-measuring models. The different steps of the microfinance process, combined with the different areas of risk, have been identified using a risk management approach. From this vantage point, the accounting and financial performance analysis become tools of risk management. Thus, performance indicators provide information that may identify potential or existing problems related to specific types of risk. This diagnosis can lead to preventive changes in risk manage-ment for those specific problem areas, which in turn may improve financial performance. This book illustrates how to measure perform-ance, and how to identify and manage microfinance risks in order to improve financial performance. Good risk management means good

performance and good performance, in the long term, means sustainability. In microfinance good performance is usually ensured by lowering the funding costs, or by charging higher fees for services. The vast majority of sustainable MFIs obtain large amounts in grants and soft loans and apply interest rates and fees that are much higher than the market rate. Most of the time increased attention to risk management can help reduce financial and operational costs by lowering the probability of substandard portfolio performance. Risk management is, thus, a prerequisite for independence from subsidies and for a more accurate pricing policy. From this perspective, risk management offers the added benefit of fostering sustainability without compromising outreach.

This book is composed of nine chapters. The first step has been to clarify the realm of modern microfinance. Chapter 1 offers a new taxonomy for microfinance in the light of the recent and future changes in the supply and demand of the microfinance market. This classification considers two main microfinance trends: international microfinance for development policies and domestic microfinance for industrialized countries.

Chapters 2 and 3 outline the main features of microfinance products, from a technical and strategic point of view. Knowledge of financial products available on the market is essential for the implementation of efficient microfinance strategies. It makes it possible to better tailor the supply to the specific target of beneficiaries served; it makes it easier to manage the risk of the MFI's portfolio. From this perspective, traditional and new products, both for individual clients and for MFIs themselves are analysed.

Before entering the core story of risk management (Chapter 5), we analysed the dichotomy that distinguishes microfinance from traditional finance, and which dramatically affects microfinance management. Chapter 4 describes the concepts of sustainability and outreach, illustrating the relationship between them and identifying the key strategies to better combine positive financial performance with ethical and social goals.

Chapter 5 enters into the field of microfinance risk management. Here, a taxonomy of microfinance risks is proposed; business, financial and process risks are explained, both with reference to their determinants and to management policies that can be implemented. Each risk is analysed considering both a single project approach and a portfolio approach.

Chapters 6 and 7 concern two main tools for risk management: process monitoring and financial performance analysis. Process monitoring is

one of the major weaknesses of MFIs, particularly for informal and semiformal MFIs. Chapter 6 describes how MFIs should design their processes, distinguishing different phases and identifying various areas of responsibility, and specifically how to implement a monitoring system. Chapter 7 describes the main issues concerning performance analysis in microfinance, offers a description of the main standards developed at the international level and proposes a new model of performance analysis, both for single microfinance programmes and for MFIs.

Chapter 8 considers two key variables for risk management: regulation and supervision. This subject matter mainly affects formal MFIs that must respect capital ratios imposed by regulatory authorities, and that must take into account the effect of capital requirements on their financial performance. The chapter also outlines the main problems concerning regulating the microfinance market and it can be a useful guide for those countries that are in the process of implementing or adopting microfinance regulatory standards.

Finally, Chapter 9 illustrates a possible future scenario for the microfinance market. This future includes the idea of projecting a microfinance financial platform strictly related to microfinance risk management and performance. Modern microfinance should be characterized by a greater cooperation among international donors and governmental bodies, both national and local, financial intermediaries and MFIs themselves. Each one of these actors can play an important role in fostering the efficiency and the efficacy of microfinance initiatives, as well as in supporting ethical sustainability. This effort must be coordinated and rationalized within a microfinance network that identifies roles and responsibilities of each actor corresponding with their skills and institutional objectives.

1

A New Conception of Microfinance

Mario La Torre

1.1 Introduction

Dealing with microfinance presents two problems today: first, its operational limits are not clearly defined and, secondly, its very nature is unclear. These issues can be summarized in two questions frequently evoked among practitioners and academics in this field: what difference is there between microfinance, the better-known microcredit and traditional finance? Does microfinance come under the heading of ethical finance?

The continuous extension of financial services offered in microfinance programmes and the ever-increasing diversification of clients extend the boundaries of microfinance well beyond the classic role of financial assistance to the 'poorest of the poor', characterized by the Grameen Bank model. Therefore, what is it that distinguishes modern microfinance from traditional finance? On what basis can we make such a distinction?

Moreover, the social and humanitarian aims behind microfinance and its channelling through non-profit organizations would lead to it being classified among the activities of ethical finance. However, the desire not to label such assistance as mere donations, as well as the increasing involvement of regulated financial intermediaries, brings microfinance closer to traditional finance. Can modern microfinance still be considered ethical finance?

This chapter addresses these problems suggesting a new taxonomy for a modern microfinance. To achieve this, it is essential first to consider the traditional features of microfinance and microcredit. Then, in light of the current trend, it is necessary to identify a new definition for microfinance in relation to the different characteristics of supply and demand.

1.2 The nature of microfinance: microfinance vs microcredit

The expression 'microfinance' most commonly denotes the offer of modest financial services to zero or low income clients. Thus, any small-scale activity characterized by limited funds and low-income beneficiaries may fall into the field of microfinance.

Traditionally, microfinance is associated with programmes that benefit clients with serious subsistence problems in developing countries. For many years microfinance overlapped with microcredit – small loans, often without traditional guarantees, aimed at improving the lives of clients and their families or at sustaining small-scale economic activities. The resources, which came mainly from funds donated by states and supranational organizations, were channelled to their recipients most often through non-governmental organizations (NGOs) and local partners (Figure 1.1).

It is, in fact, a shared procedure that NGOs and donor countries operate together with other locally-based organizations, such as municipalities or governments, or others from the third sector, which also help to facilitate the screening and management of credit positions. In order to reduce the physical, and often cultural, gap between intermediaries who provide credit and the beneficiaries of the microcredit, many institutions have recourse to a network of local promoters, known as loan officers, who visit potential clients to gather information during the selection and monitoring phases and, later, to collect instalments for loans granted.

Socio-demographic changes over the last few decades have significantly altered the world economic scene. For microfinance, the new situation has meant potential new beneficiaries, new products and a greater involvement of financial intermediaries. Exclusion from the traditional financial system, seen as the inability to access basic financial services, includes millions of people today, both in developing countries and industrialized

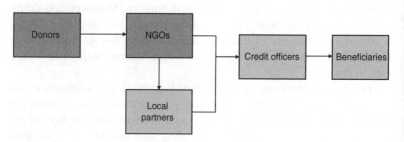

Figure 1.1 The standard microcredit structure

countries. Traditional poverty thresholds have shifted and new categories of 'poor' people have appeared, even outwith developing countries.

New beneficiaries have brought new financial needs with them. Over the past decade, new microfinance services have developed alongside microcredit. This development has also gained momentum from the observation that structured financial assistance increases the efficacy of the programmes, while at the same time improving the level of sustainability. The widening of the services on offer has taken five directions: credit products, which provide alternatives to loans, savings, insurance services, structured finance and technical assistance.

It is not surprising, therefore, that in the last few years financial intermediaries in industrialized countries have been taking greater notice of microfinance. It represents a way of reaching and gaining loyalty from new groups of clients and helps to improve corporate social responsibility.

Thus, at present, it is economic reasons, as well as concern for their public image, that spur financial intermediaries to become more involved in microfinance. All of which poses an unavoidable question: is it still possible to go back to a microfinance model that resembles the first, traditional microcredit initiatives? Do the new demographic, social and economic trends, combined with the emerging involvement of financial intermediaries, perhaps call for a review of the traditional microfinance model?

1.3 The demand for microfinance

Traditionally, those people who benefit from microfinance are citizens of developing countries who struggle to provide for themselves, known unfortunately as 'the poorest of the poor'. Within this category, women are of particular significance since they constitute the group that is most affected by financial exclusion in many developing countries. Moreover, numerous studies have shown that women are generally more capable of paying back microcredit than men and manage to invest the funding received in more profitable initiatives.

More recently, microfinance has turned its attention to self-employed workers and individuals in charge of small, often family-owned businesses, which are unable to obtain bank credit. For micro-entrepreneurs, microfinance represents an alternative to credit given by lenders, and often constitutes a way out of the money-lending system.

Thus, in the last few years microfinance has served a group of beneficiaries largely distinct from the one normally associated with microcredit. Currently, potential microfinance beneficiaries could also include

individuals who, although not living in poverty, have general difficulty in gaining access to the financial system.

In this way, modern microfinance is broadening its target from 'the poorest of the poor' to all victims of financial exclusion. The phenomenon of financial exclusion has been defined in the literature as 'the inability to access financial services in an appropriate way' (Carbo et al., 2005). Exclusion from the financial system may concern different products and services and can be due to a number of reasons. First, there is *self-exclusion* which stems, in principle, from an individual's feeling of inadequacy with regard to the conditions required by financial intermediaries; 'the poorest of the poor' come under this category. Distance from the financial system may also be due to failure of potential clients to meet creditworthiness requirements. In this case we can refer to *access exclusion*, or exclusion following a risk assessment process carried out on clients by the financial intermediaries; in this category we find 'the poor'. 'The poorest of the poor' and 'the poor' are the two categories that represent the traditional target of microfinance programmes. However, as previously mentioned, socio-demographic as well as economic changes have heightened the significance of other forms of financial exclusion and have put forward potential new microfinance beneficiaries. Exclusion from the financial system can be the consequence of exclusion from the socio-political system (*political and social exclusion*): the victims of this are, for example, immigrants or ex-convicts and those who are 'unregistered' and are, therefore, not 'bankable'. There are also individuals who cannot gain access to the financial system because they are unable to bear the costs and conditions of financial products offered. In this case, the 'disadvantaged' individuals are subject to a *condition exclusion*. Finally, a form of financial exclusion can be identified which affects customers (mainly small-scale entrepreneurs) considered 'marginal' by the intermediaries since they represent a low-value target compared with the traditional customer evaluation models (*marketing exclusion*). The 'unregistered', the 'disadvantaged' and the 'marginalized', despite their common distance from the credit system, are characterized, *ex ante*, by increasing levels of professional and managerial ability, and respective increasing levels of creditworthiness.

The categories of beneficiaries thus identified (Figure 1.2) are entitled to microfinance support as individuals or in groups. The assistance given to individuals recalls the traditional financing of sole proprietorship and micro-enterprises, whereas the support offered to groups resembles more closely the financing of associations and cooperatives.

The continuing involvement of 'unregistered', 'disadvantaged' and 'marginalized' people determines a greater complexity of the financial

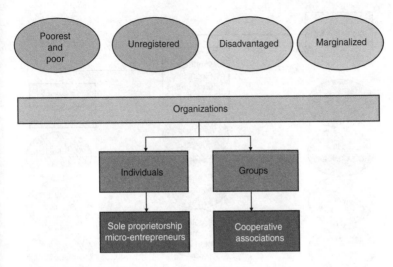

Figure 1.2 Types of microfinance beneficiaries

structure in microfinance programmes, as well as a greater involvement of financial intermediaries and, thus, a more decisive move away from the traditional patterns of microcredit.

1.4 The supply of microfinance

The institutions traditionally involved in microfinance are varied, both from an institutional point of view and as far as their aims and objectives are concerned. From a regulatory perspective, microfinance institutions (MFIs) can be classified into three main categories, depending on the regulatory thresholds of their activities: informal, semiformal and formal (Figure 1.3).

Informal institutions (self-help groups, credit associations, families, individual money lenders) do not have the status of an institution. They are providers of microfinance services on a voluntary basis and are not subject to any kind of control or regulation.

Semiformal institutions are registered entities, subject to all relevant general laws. They can be defined as microfinance financial intermediaries (MFFIs): in fact, they provide various financial services but, generally, they are not deposit-taking institutions or, if they are, they cannot grant credit, as is the case with postal savings banks. Therefore, MFFIs are subject to financial regulatory requirements, depending on their financial intermediation activities, but they are not under banking

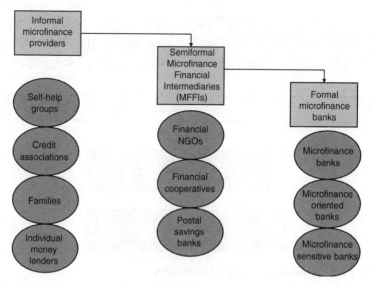

Figure 1.3 Types of microfinance institutions

regulation. Within this category it is possible to include different types of institutions with different structural and organizational complexity (financial NGOs, financial cooperatives, postal savings banks). The most popular and widespread are financial NGOs, which operate principally by offering microcredit as part of development projects, often combined with the offer of technical assistance and 'social intervention' for beneficiaries. To this aim the NGOs make use, in part or entirely, of funds donated by supranational institutions and donor states. Some of the most developed NGOs offer different types of financial services, raise private funds and take 'forced savings' from their clients.

Formal institutions can be classified into three main categories: microfinance banks (MFBs), microfinance oriented banks (MFOBs) and microfinance sensitive banks (MFSBs). They can all offer credit and they are all deposit-taking institutions: for these reasons, they are all under banking regulation.

Within MFBs it is possible to list a limited number of pure microfinance banks (PMFBs), cooperative banks and development banks.

PMFBs are banks specialized in offering only microfinance services. These may be the result of the upscaling of NGOs specialized in microcredit, which have converted to banks in order to maximize the economic sustainability of their initiatives and widen their client base.

Alternatively, such intermediaries may result from a process of privatization of public banks with the aim of providing financial support to the local community. Lastly, they may be newly created banks which decide to enter the microfinance market, attracted by the positive performances observed by intermediaries specialized in micro-enterprises.

Microfinance services can also be offered by different types of cooperative institutions which operate exclusively, or for the most part for the benefit of their own members. These include the Credit Unions in the United Kingdom and Ireland, which offer credit and other services to their own partners; the Rotating Savings and Credit Associations (ROSCAs), more widespread in developing countries, which provide rotating credit to their own members using resources from a common fund made available by the members themselves; and cooperative credit banks.[1] Despite their differences, the common characteristics of these institutions lie in the legal status of cooperative companies and in the possibility of collecting deposits, mainly through partners.

Development banks are large, centralized and usually government-owned banks created to support specific sectors (small business development banks) or geographic areas (rural development banks); in some developing countries they can also take the form of private banks.

Finally, in recent years, within formal microfinance institutions, it has been possible to include commercial banks,[2] banking groups and financial conglomerates. Here, two categories of intermediaries can be identified: microfinance-oriented banks and microfinance-sensitive banks.

In the area of microfinance-oriented banks it is possible to group together all the banks or financial institutions which are specialized in financing small to medium enterprises and micro-enterprises, and which are therefore professionally inclined to take an active part in microfinance programmes. These are mainly small, local banks, strongly rooted in the territory, and financial institutions that come directly from local bodies. Further, in the sphere of microfinance-sensitive banks it is possible to place all the banks and financial intermediaries which, for economic reasons or for their own image, view microfinance as an attractive opportunity. These consist mainly of banking groups, particularly large ones, or financial conglomerates that decide to enter into the microfinance sector (downscaling their activities), albeit to a limited extent compared with their own core business, creating specific companies or specific divisions within their organizations.

Up to now the banking system has regarded microfinance with suspicion. Traditional finance considers offering credit to individuals seen as 'unbankable', when not backed up by guarantees, as too risky. Moreover,

the process of supplying small loans incurs excessive costs owing to the significant operating costs needed to deal with each loan in relation to the amount of credit supplied. Most banks are not equipped with the methodology and professional tools suitable for microfinance, which means that, at the moment, their presence on the market is limited to a few intermediaries. However, the availability of microfinance to new categories of beneficiaries has introduced the need for new products, in addition to the existing credit, as well as better defined financing structures. Therefore, the presence of traditional financial intermediaries is likely to increase in the future. A wider participation of financial intermediaries in microfinance programmes would lead to a review of the role of NGOs and specialized institutions. Financial intermediaries can fill different roles in a microfinance programme, from simple service providers to arranger or promoter of the programmes themselves. The level of their involvement depends mainly on three factors: the legal and institutional nature, the mission and the socio-economic context in which the intermediary is working. The future scenario necessitates, thus, a new classification of practitioners that can be considered as potentially active in the microfinance sector.

1.5 Products and services in microfinance

Traditional microcredit programmes have based their success on simple structures. The progressive extension of target beneficiaries, from the category of 'poorest of the poor' to that of disadvantaged people, has brought about the need to combine credit activity with the offer of other services. This requirement is based on two main factors: on the one hand, new target beneficiaries mean new financial needs to be met; on the other hand, some categories of entrepreneur, especially disadvantaged and marginalized people, have a greater ability in organizing themselves in groups and bring about a greater complexity in the organization and running of the financed group. This, in turn, is combined with more sophisticated financial needs and calls for stricter controls by the lenders.

For these reasons it is necessary, in the field of modern microfinance programmes, to put in place a financial framework that provides other services, as well as supplying credit. These can be categorized as financial services in the strict sense or extend to services of a non financial nature (Figure 1.4). In the first case, it is possible to identify the offer of deposit taking, as well as insurance products. The need to channel the savings of beneficiaries appears stronger as the 'bankability' of the beneficiary himself increases, mainly because the percentage of the profits generated through the financial activity, and not designated to cover the subsistence

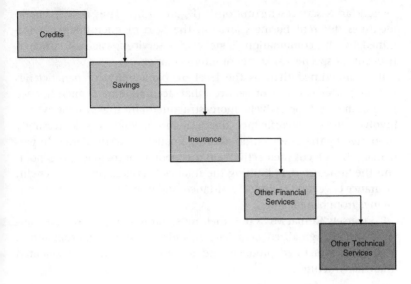

Figure 1.4 Microfinance products and services

costs of the customer, increases. Moreover, a higher rate of 'bankability' of the beneficiary generally coincides with a more structured organization which, often, outlives the project and which, to be sustainable, requires the setting up of a complete financial cycle. In this way, insurance products are also designed, on the one hand to cover the specific technical and financial risks of the project and, on the other, to be extended to the whole economic activity of the financed group.

Moreover, the organization of beneficiaries in cooperatives, or in other structured organizations, often goes with greater managerial autonomy. In such cases, the role of the investor is two-fold: to put controls in place to check respect of good governance criteria, and to provide technical assistance to the project activities. Such assistance may concern the financial and administrative management but can be extended to offering specific non-financial services. It is not uncommon, for example, that such well-organized beneficiaries need support in the commercialization and distribution of the products, in particular when the sustainability of the project requires an opening into markets outside the local context.

1.6 A new taxonomy for microfinance

In light of the classifications made, it is possible to build a matrix of modern microfinance determined by the possible combinations of

'beneficiaries–services–institutions' (Figure 1.5). The new scenario identifies different business areas in the field of microfinance determined by the combination 'beneficiaries–services', each of which is relevant for specific categories of intermediaries.

It is underlined that, as the level of 'bankability' of beneficiaries increases, the package of services that accompanies a microfinance programme is progressively more structured. In the same way, the involvement of microfinance financial intermediaries is increasingly supported by the intervention of other financial intermediaries. In particular, MFFIs focus their activity on the 'poorest of the poor', the 'poor' and the 'unregistered', limiting the financial services offered to credit, insurance cover and technical assistance, and only in few cases to forced savings from beneficiaries.

Conversely formal MFBs find their most natural targets, in 'disadvantaged' and 'marginalized' beneficiaries, and are involved in programmes with more structured products and more complex and consolidated financial structures.

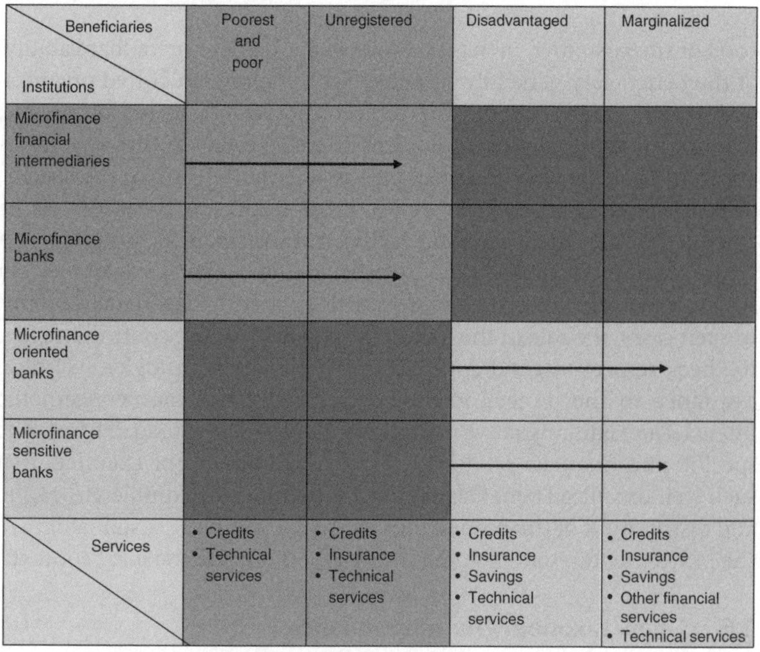

Beneficiaries / Institutions	Poorest and poor	Unregistered	Disadvantaged	Marginalized
Microfinance financial intermediaries	──────────────→			
Microfinance banks	──────────────→			
Microfinance oriented banks			──────────────→	
Microfinance sensitive banks			──────────────→	
Services	• Credits • Technical services	• Credits • Insurance • Technical services	• Credits • Insurance • Savings • Technical services	• Credits • Insurance • Savings • Other financial services • Technical services

Figure 1.5   A taxonomy for a modern microfinance

It is useful to consider, however, that in recent microfinance experience it is possible to identify a trend that highlights operating models that are not easily classifiable.

In particular, we are witnessing a cross-over movement, which is seeing a greater involvement of MFBs in programmes destined for 'the poorest of the poor', the 'poor' and the 'unregistered', and a parallel involvement of NGOs and other microfinance financial intermediaries in programmes aimed towards 'disadvantaged' or 'marginalized' beneficiaries. In fact, for microfinance-oriented banks and microfinance-sensitive banks in particular, the need to find new and more efficient ways of channelling and managing funds creates space for intervention even in programmes that are less structured, aimed at the poorest and the unregistered. At the same time the efficacy of more structured programmes is increased by the contribution of microfinance financial intermediaries (some times also microfinance providers) who contribute their local knowledge, important for improving relations between the intermediary and the beneficiary, as well as technical and operative expertise useful for the planning and monitoring of the project.

For the future, it is possible to foresee that microfinance programmes will be increasingly characterized by the presence of investors not linked to one actor but rather represent a pool of mixed institutions, which may see the presence of informal, semiformal and formal financial intermediaries at the same time.

1.7 Microfinance and ethical finance

To understand the real nature of modern microfinance, however, it is necessary to resolve a further issue: does operating in microfinance mean operating in the field of ethical finance? The issue has great relevance and cannot be resolved simply by debate. Ethical finance, indeed, has to respond to specific criteria regarding the characteristics of intermediaries and beneficiaries, the behaviour and processes adopted, as well as the products and the economic conditions applied. If an intermediary labels itself as ethical, but does not operate ethically, it carries out a process of unfair competition, liable to prosecution by national and community authorities.

It is important, therefore, to decide if microfinance is to be considered ethical finance since it is necessary, in that case, to establish the ethical parameters to be respected. Indeed, nowadays, as much in the literature as in practice, like the regulation framework of financial systems, there are no clear criteria that allow us to draw the borders of ethical finance.

Building a taxonomy of the different financial activities, which until today have been considered types of ethical finance, can help us to understand if microfinance may be included in this field.

Ethical finance can be split into three categories of activity (Figures 1.6 and 1.7): finance supporting the fight against poverty and financial exclusion (*inclusive finance*); finance that supports some sectors commonly considered ethical by collective social awareness (*selective finance*); finance that is in compliance with company regulations and associated rules which govern issues related to diligence, fairness and transparency of adopted behaviour (*compliant finance*).

In the first case, we are in the field of finance that sets itself social and humanitarian goals, and that concerns national and international donors, development banks, national governmental bodies, non-profit organizations and, in a lesser way, financial intermediaries oriented to credit. The technical form of financial support comes mainly from donations and soft loans. Microfinance comes into this category.

In the second case, financial support is given only to sectors judged ethical by the lender, based on subjective criteria that represent a common sense of good. With this approach, for example, industries such as arms, alcohol, tobacco, gambling, pornography are not financed, while investments for the environment, culture, art and social ends are

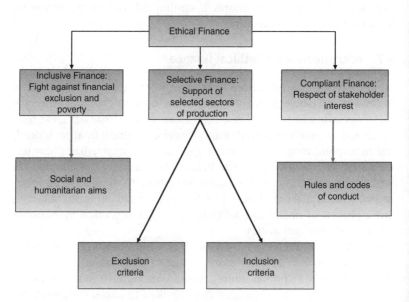

Figure 1.6 Types of ethical finance

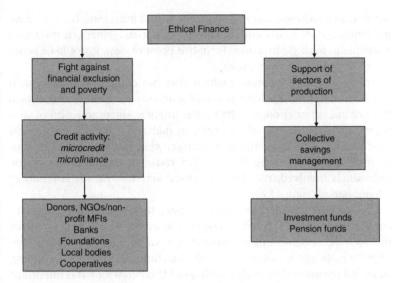

Figure 1.7   Activities and agents of ethical finance

supported. The intermediaries who follow such an approach are mainly Ethical Investment Funds (EIF), which select only ethical investments, and Ethical Pension Funds (EPF). They are institutional investors providing investment services on an individual or collective basis; none the less, over the recent years, banking intermediaries have begun to select their own credit portfolio based on the same ethical criteria. Finally, in the third case, ethics means adopting behaviour that reduces the risk of conflicts of interest between the company and the stakeholders. This approach is followed by both enterprises and financial intermediaries and non-profit organizations.

Once a classification for ethical finance has been established, it is necessary to ask oneself whether the criteria mentioned are sufficient to define the financial activities described as ethical. Certainly, financing poor women in a poor developing country is a worthy initiative, but is it enough to define as ethical even the way the funds are granted? How ethical is a bank that excludes its own customers from the sectors of arms or alcohol? If the management of a bank is against conflicts, does it mean that it must not finance the production of arms designated for the police forces? And, moreover, does fighting alcoholism mean not financing efficient winemakers and giving up our glass of wine with dinner? In the examples mentioned the degree of ethicality is so relative that finance providers can only choose sectors, companies and products

according to inclusion and exclusion criteria and must leave the subjective judgement of ethicality and, in the end, the management of their own investment, to single investors. From this point of view, it would be better to talk about selective financing.

Finally, adopting a conduct which does not come into conflict with the interests of stakeholders is surely a necessary condition for ethical finance but is not enough. A bank that finances the production of land mines but that respects all the rules in matters of transparency could hardly describe itself as ethical. Therefore, what is it that makes finance ethical? Essentially three factors, that relate to the *behaviour* of the individuals involved, the *depth* of ethical activity and the *ethicality of intermediation* (Figure 1.8).

The importance of compliance is clear in terms of the necessary conditions for ethical finance. The critical aspect in this case concerns not so much establishing whether it is right to adopt behaviour that respects rules and is not at odds with stakeholders' interests, as finding ways and means of effectively carrying out this behaviour. It is important

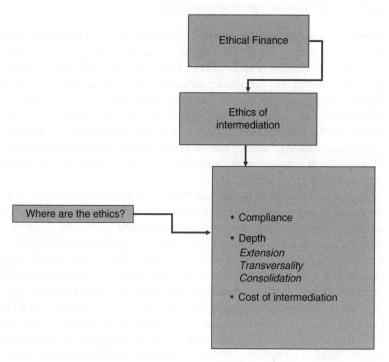

Figure 1.8   Variables of ethics in finance

that the various regulations do not remain simply an obligation but become company culture, and that ethical codes, increasingly adopted by companies, do not result in formal etiquette.

As for the depth of ethical finance, the issue is seen on three levels; *extension, transversality and consolidation*. In short, it is necessary to establish within which operating limits to extend the ethicality criteria adopted, in order to be able to use the ethical label.

Extension indicates the vertical limits of the activity; must a bank which supplies ethical loans collect ethical savings or can it finance ethical loans with traditional savings? In other words, it is necessary to clarify whether ethicality should be guaranteed for all activities, from top to bottom of the core business. Transversality indicates the horizontal limits of the activity; must an intermediary who offers other financial services, as well as providing credit, guarantee the same level of ethicality in both operating sectors? It is necessary, then, to establish whether the collateral activities of the core business should also be ethical. Finally, consolidation indicates the ethicality of the intermediary's interlocking shareholdings; can an ethical bank, which is part of a larger banking group financing the arms industry, still call itself ethical? In other words, it is necessary to clarify whether links with major shareholders or cross shareholdings should be considered in the evaluation of ethicality or whether single intermediaries should be evaluated on a stand alone basis.

The depth of ethical activity, that is to say, ethicality evaluated in terms of extension, transversality and consolidation, is an unresolved matter to which practitioners, institutions, markets and regulators still pay little attention. The setting of more precise operating limits for ethical activity would offer greater transparency to the market and would contribute to reducing the level of unfair competition from which some ethical practitioners can benefit.

The issues related to conduct and ethical depth thus deserve urgent clarification and supervision both on a national and international level. However, even more serious is the uncertainty about the third factor which adds to the definition of the ethical nature of finance: ethicality of financial intermediation. If the rules of conduct can help to increase the level of ethicality of practitioners, and the depth of the activity increases the ethicality of practitioners and programmes, what makes the intermediation process ethical? The answer is as simple as it is awkward: the cost of financial intermediation and the profit margin. No conscientious reader, even a non-expert in finance, would have difficulty in admitting that, were conditions otherwise equal, the more ethical of

two sets of loans for disadvantaged people in developing countries would be the cheapest and the one that required a lower profit margin. Likewise, it would be reasonable to believe that investors who add social and humanitarian goals to their aim of profit, and grant loans to the poor or invest in Ethical Investment Funds, are prepared to yield returns lower than those of the market, faced with the certainty of sustaining an ethical activity. However, most microcredit programmes involve intermediation costs higher than those of the market. The majority of EIFs offer returns in line with traditional funds. Why?

Microfinance cannot be grouped with donations but is characterized as an intermediation activity that rewards the will and efficiency of initiatives. The cost of intermediation and the profit margin is theoretically explained mainly by the high credit risk associated with the beneficiaries and the initiatives. Thus, a higher rate of return than that of the market average is justifiable for economic reasons. In any case, this cost is acceptable for the beneficiary since it compensates for the possibility of accessing otherwise inaccessible financial services.

Besides, with specific reference to EIFs and EPFs, market returns are often explained by the objective difficulty of selecting and monitoring ethical investments: ethical portfolios are, in most cases, made up of public shares and the shares of listed financial intermediaries, and ensure a market rate of return.

Nevertheless, when we talk about ethical finance, it is necessary to identify variables that allow us to define the financial intermediation process as ethical, and not only the agent's conduct or the activity funded. Financial intermediation consists in transferring funds from units in surplus to units in deficit. This is more efficient the safer, quicker and cheaper the transfer is. Therefore, by this definition, efficient corresponds to cheaper; it is also ethical when the intermediation cost incorporates a margin profit lower than the market rate. Encouraging access to financial services for individuals whom the financial system traditionally excludes is surely ethical; encouraging safe, quick and cheap access increases the level of ethical efficiency; fostering financial services at a price that incorporates a margin profit below market returns, and not set according to the classic risk–return relationship, makes financial intermediation ethical.

In this context, and with this definition of ethicality, it is useful to ask whether microfinance can or should be considered as ethical finance (Figure 1.9).

The aim of microfinance, linked to the fight against financial exclusion and extreme poverty, is easily classified as ethical. Likewise, it is

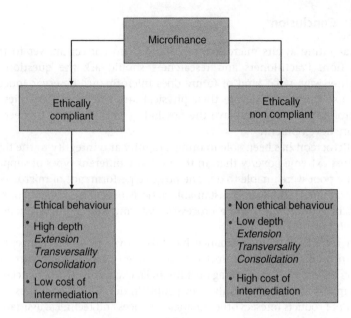

Figure 1.9 Variables of ethics in microfinance

normal to expect that practitioners of microfinance adopt ethical conduct and strive for ethicality across the range and transversality of their activity. However, to be able to define microfinance as ethical it is necessary to evaluate two aspects: consolidation and the cost of intermediation. From a strict perspective, microfinance is ethical only when it also respects a level of ethicality in consolidation and the cost of intermediation. These factors take on great relevance seen from such a perspective.

Microfinance increasingly depends on financial structures that tend to involve non-profit actors and traditional financial intermediaries at the same time, and the use of institutional resources alongside private ones. The presence of intermediaries oriented towards profit and the use of private funds can represent a risk of departure from the ethicality of consolidation and the cost of intermediation.

The choice that presents itself is therefore between 'commercial microfinance' and 'ethical microfinance'. Before giving up on ethical microfinance it is worth, then, evaluating the practicability of operating and management models for a modern microfinance that respects the ethicality criteria, without missing out on the opportunities that come from involving profit-oriented financial intermediaries and supplying private capital. This book will try to find an answer to this question.

1.8 Conclusion

What future awaits microfinance? There is no correct answer to this question. Practitioners and researchers should ask the question in another way: what kind of future does microfinance deserve? Indeed, because those who devote their physical and intellectual energies to microfinance every day have the possibility, and the duty, to steer its future development.

Microcredit has been able to bring a dignity and integrity to the fight against extreme poverty that, in the past, the different types of support to the poor were unable to do. The positive performance of microcredit programmes has allowed sustainable actions over time, capable of setting in motion worthwhile processes over and above single financial activities.

In recent years, microfinance has taken over from the concept of microcredit. The fight against extreme poverty has become part of a wider objective in the fight against financial exclusion. The beneficiaries of support are no longer only poor people in developing countries. The offer of products foresees other financial services and technical assistance, as well as microcredit. Together with donors and non-profit institutions, other microfinance institutions and traditional financial intermediaries are present on the market.

Modern microfinance therefore offers more alternatives compared with the past experience of microcredit: it is able to achieve a wider potential number of beneficiaries; it is able to suit the interventions to the effective needs and characteristics of the clients and of the selected intervention areas; and it is able to offer a more structured financial and technical assistance.

Is everything all right, then? The changes that have taken place impose the following two rules: not to diminish the positive, traditional character of microcredit; to limit the risks that financial innovation brings along with it. New customers, new products, new intermediaries: this line of development of microfinance generates more complicated financial structures than those used in the past for microcredit, new systems of evaluation and control of processes and institutions, new criteria for the objectives of performance and sustainability.

In the face of an enhanced financial sophistication, greater transparency and a more efficient management system, microfinance risks losing its real nature of immediacy and ethicality that mark its origins. Encouraging the development of microfinance, today, means especially, finding operational and managerial models able to yield balanced

cooperation between the non-profit system and the traditional financial system. The practitioners and the MFIs have to benefit from the expertise of financial intermediaries to achieve a high level of efficiency in resource management. Financial intermediaries can, with microfinance experience, regain proximity to local territories and customer care. Together, the non-profit system and the traditional financial system must collaborate to achieve the highest level of ethicality of financial intermediation for microfinance, compatible with the objectives of sustainability and performance.

2
Products and Services in Modern Microfinance

Silvia Trezza

2.1 Introduction

Compared with its original formula, the microfinance industry has evolved by expressing ever more complex needs, regarding both microfinance *beneficiaries* and *microfinance institutions* (MFIs). With reference to *beneficiaries*, the first chapter has shown how new categories of clients have emerged with an increasing degree of entrepreneurial capability; these express a demand for increasingly complex financial services, passing from the category of the 'poorest of the poor' to the 'marginal' ones. With *MFIs*, it has become ever more essential to use alternative forms of financing in respect to the donors' funds; in fact, sustainability goals impose on MFIs the need to be independent from subsidies and to access the market in order to obtain the necessary funds to carry out their business.

The microfinance industry has been, for a long time, *product driven*. In the past, the needs of the client, besides access to credit, were not fully satisfied. The request for more structured financial products and services, compared with traditional credit, imply a more complex product development process; this process must be defined starting from the objectives of the MFI and, consequently, from the identification of the target group. In other words, in modern microfinance, it is necessary that MFIs should no longer be *product driven* but *market driven*, in order to take into account the growing level of complexity of the financial needs of the beneficiaries.

Which are the factors that MFIs must take into consideration when it wants to offer new products beyond plain microcredit? When and how should they offer non-financial services? Can a single institution offer, at the same time, financial services and technical assistance or is it

necessary to create a partnership with other institutions? Finally, how can an MFI access the capital market in order to satisfy its funding needs and operate in a sustainable manner? This chapter will try to answer to these questions that have an ever greater relevance in the microfinance industry; in fact, offering *client responsive products* means pursuing objectives of sustainability through credit methodologies that help the beneficiaries in fulfilling their own contractual obligations.

2.2 Financial services

For a long time the offer of financial services to low-income clients meant the granting of microloans to develop microbusinesses. The beneficiaries of microcredit have typically been 'the poorest of the poor', the 'poor' and women, who have mainly benefited from small loans used to finance their cash flow. In the past decades microcredit projects have assumed wider features than their original ones. In modern microfinance the 'poorest of the poor' is no longer the only client. All the victims of financial exclusion have now been added to the traditional target beneficiaries. In addition to developing countries, there are now industrialized countries with high levels of financial exclusion; in addition to the non-profit institutions there is an ever-increasing number of traditional credit intermediaries.[1]

The step from microcredit to microfinance requires the effort of reconsideration of the business models and the distribution methodology of financial services. It is not by chance that many authors define the current period as the 'financial services era' and underline how the recent consideration of the variety of new financial services motivates the knowledge of an increasing complexity and variety of needs of low-income clients (Rutherford, 2003).

The poor, in fact, do not only need productive loans: they need further financial services in order to meet other specific needs. Examples are the demand for credit or savings in order to provide education for their children; the need for insurance services to deal with shock or emergency situations; the requirement for savings and insurance services to meet the costs of old age and funeral services. From this perspective, it is then possible to distinguish between the following needs:

- medium- and long-term funding needs (circulating and fixed capital);
- access to safe, fast and cheap payment systems;
- saving and liquidity needs;
- risk hedging.

Table 2.1   Financial needs and products in modern microfinance

Products Financial needs	Credit products	Saving products	Payment services	Insurance products
Short/medium-term credit	• Microcredit (working capital)			
Medium/long-term credit	• Microcredit • Microleasing • Micro venture-capital (working capital and fixed capital)			
Access to safe, fast and cheap payment systems			• Money transfers • Credit cards • Smart cards	
Saving and liquidity needs		• Voluntary products (demand deposit, contractual products, time deposits, equity products) • Compulsory saving products		
Risk hedging				• Microinsurance

Such needs can be met by using the typologies of financial services that are typically considered in the studies of financial intermediation:

- credit products;
- savings products;
- payment services;
- insurance products.

In Table 2.1 the links between the main needs of the low-income client, services and financial products are represented in a needs/products matrix. Starting from such classification, the sections that follow analyse the main characteristics of the financial products typically offered by modern microfinance. Finally, it is necessary to point out that the financial services are often associated to non-financial services of technical assistance. These are examined in section 2.4.

2.2.1   Credit products

The most common credit products in microfinance are microcredit and microleasing. The first is offered mainly for circulating capital needs and, rarely, for needs in the medium to long term; the second is for

lasting needs. Some of recent experiences of micro-venture-capital can also be added to credit products.

Microcredit

The idea that a loan of a modest size can help the poorest to escape their condition is credited to Muhammad Yunus and the experience of the Grameen Bank, thanks to which millions of poor have benefited from small loans to support their businesses. Beginning with this experience, different lending methodologies were born, each of which works well if correctly chosen in relationship to the needs and characteristics of the clients served, the external environment and the organizational structure.

Granting credit to disadvantaged populations implies sustaining significant costs linked to the difficulty in evaluating the risks, the asymmetric information and the lack of guarantees. To manage credit risk it is necessary to have a good relationship between borrower and lender. This relationship must be based on reciprocal trust, something that requires a reasonable proximity between the two parties. For this reason, historically, microfinance services are offered by non-profit institutions, mainly NGOs, since these can ensure a more direct contact with the local community compared with financial institutions.

The main characteristics of microcredit are summarized in Table 2.2. The loans paid out, above all, used to finance cash flow are of limited amounts. Loan amount varies depending on the beneficiaries' use of the

Table 2.2 Main features of microcredit

Loan size:	Limited (from tens of euros to a few thousand, depending on the geographic area).
Financed assets:	Working capital (more rarely fixed assets).
Loan terms:	6–18 months.
Frequency of repayments:	Monthly or weekly.
Credit worthiness analysis:	Based mainly on qualitative considerations.
Distribution channel:	Mainly through networks of local promoters.
Risk mitigation:	Carried out through self-selection solidarity groups and with progressive criteria in the amounts paid out.
Sustainability:	Different levels of sustainability, mainly achieved through interest rates higher than the market rate.
Quality of portfolio:	In some countries higher than that of the traditional banking sector.

loan and the debt capacity of the borrower. In the group lending method-ology the loan amount is usually between 50 and 100 euros. Individual loans, however, are characterized by higher amounts, even to the order of several thousand euros. The frequency of loan payments, normally weekly or monthly, depends on the production cycle of the microbusiness (e.g. seasonal businesses or businesses that generate regular revenue) as well as on the management criteria of the MFI. With reference to this last aspect, the frequency of payments tends to increase as it becomes more difficult for the moneylenders to reach the borrowers. Loan term varies from six to 18 months, according to the needs of the customer and his debt capacity.

The lending methodology in microfinance differs widely from that of traditional finance. The credit worthiness analysis, for example, focuses exclusively on qualitative factors; traditional guarantees are absent and often substituted by solidarity groups. The distribution channel is mainly dealt by local promoters. This is a *modus operandi* that is far from the stan-dards of traditional banking intermediaries, who require guarantees and accounting documentation to grant loans. Also for this reason, the role of commercial banks in microfinance is still limited, due, among other things, to the high operating costs that a credit management on a small scale requires. Therefore, microfinance industry has developed different methods of credit delivery. It is possible to distinguish between two main categories: individual loans and group loans (Figure 2.1).

Individual lending models are more similar to those of banks. The guar-antees required are collateral attached to low-value tangible assets owned by the beneficiary. In some cases the loan is guaranteed by the presence of a guarantor, a third party who undertakes to repay the loan if the borrower fails to do so. The MFIs should be able to evaluate the

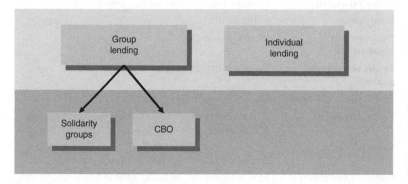

Figure 2.1 Group loans vs individual loans

debt capacity of the microentrepreneur and the client's cash-flow. Such analysis rarely utilizes a particularly formal and precise procedure; consequently, it is the responsibility of the credit officers, as experts on the local territory, to go to the client and pay visits and informal interviews, in order to acquire the necessary information. This 'door to door' activity allows the credit officer to proceed with the compilation of the paperwork required for the analysis of the beneficiary's creditworthiness. The paperwork is nevertheless less formal than that used by banks.[2] The acquaintance of credit officers with microentrepreneurs is very important even after the loan has been issued, in order to monitor constantly how the loan is used and the growth possibilities of the existing business.

In any case, these forms of loans, supported by individual guarantees, are particularly appropriate in an urban context, with microbusiness clients able to develop structured businesses. The advantage of this method consists in the flexibility of the supplied amounts and the payment schedule adapted to the actual needs of the client. The main limit is the exclusion of the category of the 'poorest' and the 'poor', due to the lack of sufficient assets to guarantee the loans. For this reason this approach is mostly suitable for projects that aim to reduce financial exclusion and focus on beneficiaries that fall into the category of 'disadvantaged' and 'marginalized' who live in areas or countries with more advanced economies.

Group-based lending has its main advantages in overcoming the need for collateral; these are substituted by a mechanism of peer pressure from other group members as a repayment incentive. The failure to repay the loan by one component of the group of beneficiaries, in fact, determines the refusal to grant further loans to the other members and generates mutual monitoring by each member on the other. With this system another typical problem of the credit process is reduced: through peer monitoring there is a reduction of transaction costs and the imperfect information that characterizes the relationship between lender and borrower. The groups are formed in a spontaneous manner by people belonging to the same community; in this way the deep mutual knowledge allows for an accurate selection at low cost to the beneficiaries.[3] For this reason, this approach is most effective for microfinance projects in support of beneficiaries that fall into the category of 'poorest', 'poor' and 'unregistered', situated in non-urban geographic settings and in developing countries.

Group lending presents different characteristics. The main models can be divided into solidarity groups and community-based-organizations (CBOs).

The difference between the two models is that in the first case the loans are granted to the individuals and are guaranteed by the group that maintains a constant relationship with the MFI and does not develop a self-management financial capability. In the second case the loan is granted to the group that manages independently the funds received from the MFI, distributing them between members and becoming in the medium term an independent institution. Examples of solidarity-group lending methodologies are the Latin-American model and the Grameen model; village banking, revolving loan fund and savings and loan associations are approaches that fall within CBOs.

Microleasing

Leasing is a contract with which one party (the lessor), in exchange for the payment of a regular instalment, concedes to another (the lessee) the use of equipment. The leasing contract carries out the function of satisfying financial requirements that arise from investment decisions. The fundamental requirement of the contract lies in the existence of an asset that is useful to the client and suited to the location.

Low-income customers are not always able to sustain the cost of investments. Microleasing, therefore, allows them to obtain the availability of the asset without having to tie up capital equal to the whole value of the goods, since the asset itself remains the property of the lessor. Therefore, microleasing is useful to microfinance when there is a need to support the beneficiary not only by financing his cash flow, but also the fixed asset required for the business. In microfinance, microleasing contracts present different characteristics depending on the social and economic background.[4]

Micro-Venture-Capital

Derived from traditional finance, micro-venture-capital consists in funding to start-up microbusinesses with the objective of supporting their development in the medium and long term. Micro-venture-capital is, therefore, an instrument that implies risk sharing by the lender: thus, it is formally different from classic methods of financial support through credit. Nevertheless, in the case of microfinance, the venture capitalist has a different role than that covered in traditional finance (Box 2.1). In particular, international donors could assume the role of venture capitalists without changing their own essence. Actually, the donations themselves (grants and subsidies) could be transformed into risk capital. In the event of a negative performance of the projects supported, the loss of capital would be treated as a free donation. In the event of a

---

Box 2.1   Fundusz Mikro's experience

In 1994, the Polish American Enterprise Fund established Fundusz Mikro. Fundusz Mikro began its lending operations in February 1995; in 2001, it began offering a new product to assist long-term clients with larger business development and improvement investments. The Micro Venture Capital (MVC) loans are given to stable customers in at least their third year of borrowing and are processed on a group basis. Fundusz Mikro offers a long-term cooperation with its clients in the form of start-up loans, loans for microbusinesses operating in rural areas, and loans for associations created for small investment for the community.

---

successful outcome, the repayment of the risk capital could be put into circulation for new microfinance projects supported by the donor. Venture capital is a practical route for offering, with donations also, the capability of instilling financial responsibility into the borrower, in the same manner as happens with microcredit, and overcoming the policy of aid that does not respond to the principles of modern microfinance. Naturally, owing to its characteristics, venture capital is more suited to programmes in support of the 'disadvantaged' and 'marginalized'.

2.2.2   Saving services

Saving mobilization is an important tool in microfinance, both for MFIs and the clients. For MFIs the collection of the savings represents a fundamental instrument in achieving sustainability. Indeed, saving mobilization allows clients to obtain the resources to finance the growth of the loan portfolio and, consequently, to become independent from subsidies or external financing. For the poor and, more generally, for financially excluded people, access to deposit services allows them to manage emergencies and to meet expected expenses, such as education, marriage ceremonies, old age and death.

Microbusiness incomes are often uncertain and irregular, something that implies difficulties in acceding to types of credit that require fixed regular repayments. In these cases, savings represent a fundamental instrument in the management of temporary imbalances in the microbusinesses. Furthermore, the majority of the poor receive flows of remittances from their families living in urban areas or abroad; access to deposit services is, therefore, necessary in order to keep these payments secure. In microfinance the demand for saving deposits acts with the same motivation that characterizes the formal system: savings are, in fact, the money saved today to be spent in the future for the needs of the family

and for businesses. Access to deposit products allows for the safe storage of money; it also represents a source of revenue, given the rates of interest paid on savings deposits. The poor, and more generally the financially excluded, have demonstrated a potential capacity to generate savings. The informal system has always played a major role in saving mobilization. In developing countries, for example, there are a lot of informal operators: moneylenders, savings clubs, rotating savings and credit associations, family and neighbour networks. However, these informal mechanisms, which have for a long time represented the only savings alternative for the poor, are very expensive, both in terms of high risks and low or negative interest rates.

Microfinance has dedicated particular attention to saving, and many MFIs have begun to collect savings under various forms. In general, it is possible to distinguish between compulsory savings and voluntary savings. *Compulsory saving products* consist of mechanisms of forced saving, which imply that a certain percentage of the supplied loan is held back and placed in a fund that acts as a guarantee. In the majority of cases, the clients are able to use their savings at the end of the loan cycle. For these reasons, such products are often perceived by the clients as a sort of 'entry fee' to accede to the loan more than as a savings product itself (Ledgerwood, 2000).

Nevertheless, the poor normally prefer *voluntary saving products*. These are volunteer methods of saving collection that allow the saver to deposit and withdraw, with varying frequency and expiry dates, according to the products' liquidity. The main typologies are demand deposits, contractual deposits, time deposits and equity products.

Demand deposits and current accounts represent the contractual forms to which low-income clients refer in order to manage liquidity. The reasons for this are mainly related to their features, which make the use of savings particularly easy and flexible. There is, in fact, no restriction on the deposit management in terms of cashing in and withdrawals, which can be made on every due date.

Contractual products are used to meet the expected needs (Box 2.2); the client deposits the established sums on a scheduled basis for a specific period of time, after which he can reclaim all the funds paid in, plus interest. These products ensure lower liquidity and higher revenue than demand loans, which allow the accumulation of small sums of money for planned future expenses. The predictability of the cash flow implies that the products are easier to manage for MFIs rather than demand products.

Time deposits allow for the deposit and withdrawal of large sums of money for expected needs. They allow the customer to deposit a certain

---

Box 2.2 Buro Tangail's 'Contractual Saving Agreement'

Buro Tangail in Bangladesh developed a simple contractual savings account in 1997. This savings product involved a five-year contractual savings agreement. The savings are deposited on a weekly or monthly schedule selected by the client. The scheme has proven immensely popular. In 2004 70 per cent of Buro's customers voluntarily elected to open a contractual savings account. From 1997 to 2004 205 860 long-term contractual savings accounts were opened.

Source: <www.microfinancegateway.org>

---

sum once, for a set term. The demand for these products, however, is rare; apart from small farmers in the winter, the poor are rarely able to save large sums of money.

Finally, *equity products* represent a typical savings instrument of Credit Unions, self-help groups and financial service associations. The members invest savings in these institutions; in exchange they receive periodic dividends and the possibility of accessing greater amounts through loans.

The supply of saving services requires the consideration of many factors. Regarding MFIs, for example, the supply of voluntary savings products requires complex internal control systems and management information systems, as well as careful liquidity management under the prudential regulation rules; therefore, they are typical products of formal MFIs. Compulsory savings, on the other hand, fall into the informal framework, because technically they represent forms of guarantee for loans and they can be also offered by semi-formal MFIs. Savings mobilization, therefore, requires the consideration of a whole series of other factors linked to the regulatory context. In the majority of countries the collection of savings is reserved to the banking system, with the consequence that a number of institutions (informal and semi-formal MFIs) involved in microfinance do not have the capability to collect savings and issue loans (lending activity). In this regard, the lack of an adequate regulatory framework to sustain microfinance has led many MFIs to transform themselves into banks, as in the case of the Grameen Bank and the BancoSol in Bolivia.

2.2.3 Payment services

Alongside savings and loan products, a limited number of MFIs have begun to offer payment services also. These are included in a category of financial services that the poor request in order to have the possibility of transferring money through secure channels. The demand for such

services mainly derives from those categories of clients that have a greater managerial ability (e.g. 'marginal' clients) and those that need to perform transactions through alternative means to cash – often associated with deposit products – such as cheques, bank transfers and credit and debit cards. Recently some MFIs have begun to offer credit cards, debit cards and smart cards.[5] Those who demand payment services are also the most marginal sectors, which have the need to transfer payments to and from family members through more secure channels than informal ones, such as families and friends.

In microfinance, therefore, the demand for payment services arises – considering the necessary exceptions – through the specific needs of banking clients: safety, availability and accessibility to payment instruments, fast and cheap settlement. The MFIs that offer payment services are not, so far, numerous because of the complexity of the infrastructure and the technology that payment systems require. For such reasons, and for the stability and monetary policies, the monetary function is still the prerogative of the banking industry and, in part, of the postal system. Such circumstance often makes the partnership between MFIs and banks necessary.

2.2.4 Insurance products

The demand for health and loan insurance derives from the need of low-income customers to limit and cover the risks in case of death or loss of assets. Microinsurance products, drawn up to reduce uncertainty and its effects, represent a fundamental instrument in microfinance, given the vulnerability of the poor to risk. Natural disasters, health problems of the beneficiary, or death of livestock, are all events that can be dealt with by microinsurance. The product and process risks, which characterize microfinance, do find in insurance cover an important management solution.[6]

From the 1990s a large number of MFIs have shown a growing interest in offering insurance products for their own low-income clients (Box 2.3). The reasons for this interest are to be found, other than the need to protect the poor from risk, in the opportunity for MFIs to reduce the levels of default on loans by offering these products. The most widely available insurance products in microfinance are health and life insurance, livestock and crop insurance and compulsory insurance against loan default.

Microinsurance is not always the best solution for reducing the vulnerability of the poor to risks and to improve the quality of the loan portfolio. Insurance is a high risk business; in developed countries this is

Box 2.3   FINCA International's insurance products

Operating with the village banking methodology, FINCA International is a non profit organization present in 19 different countries. Under a partnership with the American International Group (AIG) in Uganda, FINCA started to provide life and disability insurance. This is designed to provide protection not only to clients but also to the institution, should the client be involved in a debilitating accident or should the client die in the course of the loan cycle. The insurance products are provided under a partnership model: AIG provides the insurance services, while FINCA provides AIG with the names of its clients and up to three of their family members.

Source: <www.microfinancegateway.org>

limited to insurance companies or to financial intermediaries used to managing a single portfolio of numerous, similar, risks. In developing countries, many MFIs operate at the limits of legality, this being due to an unfavourable legal and regulatory context and/or the inability of many MFIs to define and successfully manage microinsurance schemes. These aspects show how it is very often advisable to create partnerships with formal insurance providers, rather than offering microinsurance products directly. These partnerships present various advantages for formal insurers as well as for MFIs. The insurers can gain access to new markets, MFIs can benefit from the expertise of formal institutions in defining client responsive products, without having to spend time and resources in the design phase of the product.[7] On the other hand, offering insurance products directly involves incurring greater risks, especially if the insurance side of the business is not separate from the savings and credit side. Furthermore, directly offering insurance products requires different skills from those required for credit or saving supply, for example, setting premiums, forecasting losses, etc. Finally, the MFI can incur more moral hazard problems (Brown, 2003).

2.3   Product development process

The awareness of new financial needs, also in relation to new categories of beneficiaries, has imposed the need to define new financial products and services on a *systematic process* basis. The majority of MFIs have dedicated little attention to the product development process, mainly offering *working capital loans* in order to finance microbusinesses. For a long time, microloans were distributed through credit methodologies (solidarity groups, village banking, etc.) characterized by untraditional mechanisms of beneficiaries' screening, monitoring of the borrower's

actions and incentives to repay the loan. These features, drawn up to manage the risks related to the offering of financial services to the disadvantaged, were often found to be unsuitable for further application in other socioeconomic contexts and poorly adapted to satisfy the variety of clients' financial requirements. In stepped lending methodology, for example, the low size of the initial loan was not always adequate in respect of the real financial needs of the microentrepreneur.

In the same way, the credit methodologies based on solidarity groups did not satisfy the needs of all the beneficiaries, especially those microentrepreneurs with expanding businesses. Again, the intensification of the relationship between client and MFI has generated the demand for new financial services and a greater variety and quality of products. Consequently, as the microfinance industry evolves and the level of competition increases, MFIs need to redefine their products or develop new ones, following a *market driven* and a more *client responsive* approach. This implies a systematic product development process that takes into consideration the objectives of the MFI, the demands of the target client and the existence of other financial services providers.

Many MFIs, until now, have followed a top-down approach to product development, characterized by the almost total absence of market research, an inadequate costing/pricing of the product, and the lack of pilot testing and a planned roll-out (Wright et al., 2001). Before placing a new product on the market, it is necessary to verify that there is a demand for that product, that the product is profitable for the MFI, that the new product will be supported by an adequate monitoring and reporting system and, finally, that the staff have been specifically trained for the management and sale of the new product. Therefore, an MFI that decides to offer fixed asset loans alongside working capital loans, will need to define new procedures of credit evaluation and implement a new management information system. Neglecting such aspects in redefining a financial product or in the creation of a new one can, in the long term, have serious consequences in terms of an increase in the drop-out rate, in the loss of a competitive edge and, therefore, in performance and sustainability. There are examples of many MFIs lending groups that began to offer individual loans without preliminary cash flow analysis of their clients.

The process of product development is a dynamic process that requires time and resources, both human and financial. Brand (2001) defines the product development process as a 'systematic step by step approach to developing or refining existing products'. This process is

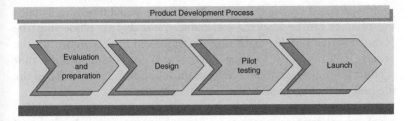

Figure 2.2   Product development process

made up of the following steps: evaluation and preparation; design and development; pilot testing and product launch (Figure 2.2). It is obvious that each of these phases is influenced by three fundamental factors: institutional strength, and customer's needs and competitors. A change in any one of these factors brings about the need to re-examine each phase of the process.

The *evaluation and preparation* phase represents the preliminary phase in the process, during which the MFI has to evaluate the viability of offering a new product or whether to proceed instead with the modification of an existing one. This evaluation must be carried out beginning with the analysis of the institutional capacity of the MFI and the market situation. Therefore, an MFI that wishes to place a new financial product on the market must first of all consider that the organizational structure, the risk-management and information systems, its human resources and the institutional culture are suited to the characteristics of the new product. The second phase (*design and development*) consists of defining a product prototype that will subsequently be tested in the pilot-testing phase. The definition of this product must be preceded by market research, a main part of the product development process since it allows the analysis of the financial needs of the client to be carried out from different kinds of information (for example, loan officers or consultative groups).

When the product prototype is defined, it is necessary to pass onto the *pilot-testing phase*, through which the prototype is offered to a limited group of beneficiaries in order to evaluate whether the characteristics of the product respond to real client needs. Pilot testing represents a fundamental phase in the process as it allows the MFI to verify the real demand for that product and its potential success. If the pilot testing has a positive outcome, or rather if the product is accepted, the next phase in the process can be reached. If the testing of the prototype fails, it will be necessary to take a step back in the process and redefine a better

prototype based on the information obtained through testing. Finally, the product can be *launched and commercialized*. This phase must be planned with a suitable marketing strategy. Even in this phase, like the others, it is necessary to have internal systems to support the new product line and the human resources must be adequately trained in the methods of management and sale of the product.

Offering products and services on the basis of a systematic product development process takes up time and resources, both human and financial. However, it also represents an opportunity to better service the market demand and to exploit the advantages created by changes in the market. The process of product development needs, therefore, greater attention by both MFIs and by donors. For MFIs, offering client-responsive products means reducing the number of drop-outs, increasing the quality of the credit portfolio, attracting a growing number of new customers and consequently contributing to the long-term viability of the MFI. For donors, supporting client responsive financial institutions means acquiring knowledge on the importance of the product development process and supporting those MFIs that have the institutional capacity to develop new products.

2.4   Non financial services: minimalist vs integrated approach

In the previous sections we took into consideration the needs and the financial products of modern microfinance. Alongside financial services the majority of microfinance projects also offer technical assistance services to microentrepreneurs. These are services offered to support microfinance clients in the start-up and development of their microbusiness. In some cases, especially in the development cooperation programmes, these services have the objective of preparing group members to contact the MFI and establish a solid and long-lasting relationship. These services represent a preliminary support. In other cases, these services have the objective of contributing to the development of the economic microbusinesses through business training, production training or marketing and technology services. Often, these services are aimed at assisting the beneficiaries with the sale and commercialization of their products. Small producers, in fact, do not always have links with the market and their products may not find an outlet. In these cases, the MFI organizes the sales network for the sale of the product.

In the best microfinance projects, these services are supported by offering different types of training courses to the beneficiaries, from

management to accounting and also marketing to provide the beneficiary with the necessary abilities to better manage his microbusiness. Very often, microfinance programmes also include, alongside the microcredit component, social services focused on improving the living conditions of the target group. Typically, these are training courses on health, nutrition and education. Technical assistance services can be offered by a wide range of institutions that operate in partnership with the MFIs, such as universities, training institutions, networks, government agencies and non-profit sector institutions. Frequently, the MFI themselves offer non financial services. In these cases, it is necessary that the management and the bookkeeping of these products is kept separate from that of financial services.

The distribution of development services for businesses requires subsidies, since it is not a fee-based service. This raises important questions regarding the evaluation of the social impact of the service and the measurement of the performance of the MFI.

The decision to offer non financial services, as well as financial services, depends on the objectives of the MFI and on its capacity to attract donors' funds in order to sustain the costs involved. In literature and in operational methods, we distinguish between the minimalist and integrated approach, depending on whether the MFI limits itself to offering only financial services or not.

2.5   New frontiers in microfinance services

The microfinance industry is being rapidly transformed. New needs emerge, not only from the beneficiaries but also from the MFIs. The previous sections have analysed the financial products and services that the modern microfinance industry has begun to offer to new categories of beneficiary. The managerial requirements of MFIs have changed in recent years and MFIs see the need to find new management techniques in financial innovations. The intensification of competitive pressures and the scarcity of donors' funds enhance the need for MFIs to find alternative financial sources beyond donations and subsidies, as well as greater management efficiency. How can a MFI access the capital market in order to satisfy its need of funding to operate in a sustainable manner?

Some innovative financial instruments have been experimented in microfinance. Though not numerous, these represent an opportunity for MFIs to have access to market funds. An innovative example is represented by the venture capital funds in support of MFIs. The Dutch Hivos-Triodos Fund (HTF) has recently launched the first venture capital

fund for microfinance in India. The fund is a Public Private Partnership between the Hivos Foundation and Triodos Bank and will focus on providing finance to India's most innovative small and medium-size microfinance institutions.[8] The collection of funds from the capital market can also be achieved through socially responsible mutual funds. These can be divided into *screened mutual funds* and *shared return funds*. The first invest primarily in socially responsible companies, the second are owned by the members of MFIs (Ledgerwood, 2000).

An interesting development in access to the capital market and risk management can be represented by asset-backed securitization, through which the MFI sells a portfolio of assets to an external company (Special Purpose Vehicle – SPV). The SPV will fund the acquisition of the assets by issuing and placing rated notes (ABSs) for an amount equivalent to the value of the transferred assets. The classic operation requires, in fact, the packaging of a basket of credits from the assets of the originator and its transferral to a SPV which, in order to finance the purchase, issues notes that are then placed on the market. Through this technique, MFIs can manage the typical risks of financial intermediation, in particular the liquidity and credit risks. Asset securitization, indeed, allows for gathering the financial resources (liquidity) on the capital markets in exchange for the sale of part of the microloans held by the MFI. Furthermore, the securities incorporate the risk of the original credit which is, therefore, transferred from the MFI to the capital market and, thereby, to the investors in ABSs. Securitization of credit can represent a valid alternative to traditional collection systems for various reasons: alternative funding, transferral of credit risk and diversification of the credit portfolio, in the case where it is highly concentrated in certain geographical areas or in certain categories of beneficiary. Although the benefits that the operation brings are important, the costs can be substantial. The planning and the monitoring of a securitization operation are complex, mainly due to the large number of parties involved and the significant number of transactions that must be carried out. For this reason, asset securitization is viable for those MFIs that manage significant loan portfolios and that can count on the assistance of traditional financial intermediaries in the planning phase and in the placing of the notes.

2.6   Conclusion

In recent years, numerous successful experiences in the field of microfinance have contributed to spreading the idea that the improvement of living standards of the poorest can be realized not just through small

loans for production requirements, but also through a wide range of financial services.

Modern microfinance has begun to offer more sophisticated products compared with simple microcredit in response to the more complex needs of the new target clients. For MFIs, offering financial services to marginal clients means reviewing the product development process through a *market driven* approach, which takes into account the real needs of the target client. It also means supporting the collaboration between different kinds of institutions, through the formation of partnerships that, by combining different skills, allow the poor to have access to the financial system in a lasting and sustainable way. The current revolution in the microfinance sector provides, therefore, various challenges: organizational and procedural changes become necessary to increase the institutional strength of MFIs and, consequently, their capacity to access capital markets. The need to have access to alternative forms of financing, rather than donations, imposes upon MFIs the need to operate according to market and transparency schemes also in planning and implementing the products offered.

3
The Main Features of Microcredit
Gianfranco Vento

3.1 Introduction

In the world of microfinance, microcredit occupies a special place for more than a reason. First of all, it represents the most diffuse and significant product supplied by the vast majority of MFIs. Second, among all microfinance products, microcredit seems to have a greater and more direct impact on the conditions of beneficiaries, given that it allows, by using a small amount of money, to foster economic initiatives revenue-producers. Last, the supply of credit, even if of small amount, is a risky business for MFIs and, thus, it needs a particular attention in order not to incur serious loan losses.

Microcredit features, however, cannot be investigated only in one single way because of the wide and deep differences existing in the approaches carried out in different regions and by different typologies of institutions. The abundant literature concerning microcredit is characterized by particularly focusing on the on-field experiences, successful or ineffective, developed by heterogeneous institutions in different countries, by following very different lending approaches and methodologies. The study of the best practices, as well as the investigation of the major critical points of past programmes, appears surely useful in orienting those who are involved in microfinance towards more effective and efficient solutions. Nevertheless, also taking into account the essential diversities existing in different microfinance programmes, it seems to lack a managerial approach that critically examines all the most significant elements that must be found in a microcredit programme.

The absence of a comprehensive description of microcredit is due to the non-existence of a widely agreed definition of what microcredit is.

As stated in Chapter 2, microcredit cannot be included in one single definition, because it varies significantly in the aims, in the delivery methodologies and in the credit process approaches. Therefore, this chapter aims to highlight the most significant features of microcredit, in order to deepen the peculiar aspects that have distinguished until now microcredit from other financial tools focused on reducing financial exclusion, and to concentrate on the features that should be considered for the success of a microfinance programme. The considerations developed here are coherent with an approach oriented to maximize the recoveries of allocated microcredit, in order to ameliorate the financial performance of MFIs over time. Obviously, this is not the only possible scheme in microcredit, due to the presence of institutions that prioritize working with the 'poorest of the poor' rather than aiming for financial performance and sustainability.

The present chapter is structured as follows. Section 3.2 provides a brief description of the process of evaluation of beneficiaries. The following section looks at the nature of financed assets in a typical microcredit programme. The distinguishing features of microcredit, compared to traditional loans, are discussed in section 3.4, whereas section 3.5 points out the peculiarity of collateral policies. The final section looks at the interest rate policy in microcredit, which is still one of the most debated subjects so far. Section 3.7 concludes.

3.2   The screening of beneficiaries

The evaluation process of beneficiaries is a pivotal issue for the success of a microfinance programme, and therefore for the survival of MFIs.[1] Similarly to what happens for traditional financial intermediaries, the screening of clients should be anticipated by a *portfolio allocation analysis*, according to the nature of demand of microcredit in the context in which the MFI operates or in those it wishes to enter. In this preliminary phase, MFIs are required to identify the target group, or groups, they want to finance. This initial screening consists of addressing the financial resources to a limited group which, more than others, is supposed to maximize the return on investments, or, more generally, the social benefits. The size of the target group, as well as the number of groups, depends on the size of MFIs, and, moreover, on the size of the loan portfolio.

The loan portfolio composition must also follow the *principles of risk diversification*, which is not an easy task for MFIs, especially small ones.[2] Moreover, since the majority of MFIs depend – at different levels – on funds

that proceed from third-party stakeholders, the decisions of MFIs regarding allocation are often influenced significantly by the organizations that provide funding, in respect of the category of subjects that should receive financing.

At the same time, MFIs need to highlight the *purpose of microcredit*. In this regard the goal of MFIs should be to opt for those investments run by members of the target group that have the highest internal rate of return. Often the scope of microcredit is also to insert in the productive process the goods that may increase the productivity of microfirms of beneficiaries. Sometimes, the choice made by some MFIs to finance assets that result in being useful for the improvement of life conditions of beneficiaries must be considered while also taking into account the debt capacity of those borrowers. In all cases in which the repayment of microloans is in doubt, owing to the lack of a productive process, it is likely that microcredit is not the most appropriate tool to adopt.

Thus, once the population of potential customers is identified, MFIs are required to screen those who have a higher capability to use the money to produce marketable goods and services. This process is usually run in a different way, depending on several variables. However, we propose here a prototype of selection mechanism based on three main elements. The first feature for the success of a screening process is the proximity of *the net of credit officers* with the customers. The underlying idea of this is that in the population of beneficiaries there is a percentage of people which has valid entrepreneurial ideas that could be viable, but they lack funds to finance their projects. Therefore, an excellent net of credit officers allows MFIs to gather the necessary information concerning the chance of success of the different economic initiatives to support, as well as to be more conscious of the attitude of their borrowers to repay the microloans and to avoid the misuse of funds.

The creation of a net of credit officers, however, represents one of the most significant costs in a microfinance programme and, consequently, there is a trade-off between, on one hand, the number of credit officers, their qualities and skills, and, on the other, the costs of these workers. Moreover, the wideness of the net of credit officers depends also on the degree of territorial dispersion of potential beneficiaries, as well as on the incidence of labour cost. In all those cases where the potential borrowers are concentrated in a few close villages, a smaller number of credit officers can easily screen and monitor them.

Second, *the governance of MFIs* represents a key variable for the success of a microcredit programme. In fact, in environments in which there is a high degree of poverty and financial exclusion, it is likely that

those who are called to select the borrowers and to monitor them may have their own interests and priorities, which probably may not correspond with those of MFIs. Therefore, for the achievement of a good screening, MFIs have to build a coherent system of controls based on different levels and are required to set up incentive systems that can award the most efficient officers.

The third element for the success of the screening mechanism in microcredit is the adoption of *recognized and standardized procedures* for selecting the credit demands. The idea that one of the main advantages of microcredit, compared with usual credit, is the high degree of flexibility, does not have to be confused with the adoption of unusual techniques in evaluating the feasibility of a business, as well as the borrower's will to repay. Nevertheless, given that in microcredit the number of applications for a loan is usually high and the amount lent is small, top MFIs have decided to adopt a simplified version of usual credit scoring models, such as CAMEL.[3]

Thus, the analysis of credit quality in microcredit is based both on quantitative and qualitative elements, where the first emphasize the projections on production and sales – owing to the lack, in many developing countries, of historical official data on small businesses to be financed and on the track record of the borrower – whereas the second should include all those intangible aspects, such as the personal qualities of the borrower. Whatever is the blend of qualitative and quantitative elements chosen by MFIs, it is crucial for the success of the borrowers' selection process to fix *ex ante* the relative weight of both aspects.

3.3 The nature of financed assets

It has already been stated that microcredit provides best results when the borrowers are self-employed or small firms that have some valid entrepreneurial skills – such as good productive capability, marketable products, access to market, etc. – but lack capital. Therefore, even if MFIs can theoretically finance a very wide set of assets, attention is often addressed to those productive factors deficient in the production process of the borrowers, or are necessary for the start-up of new businesses.

On the other hand, the goal of a microfinance programme is to support microfirms by using small loans, which can contribute significantly to improving the productive process. Thus, the allocation process of MFIs should be oriented to finance those goods and services that, once inserted in the productive mechanism, can increase the output more than others and, consequently, the borrowers' returns.

Moreover, regarding the nature of the firms to be financially supported, these are mainly agricultural or manufacturing microenterprises, which are both labour intensive activities, but are significantly different in the timing of the productive processes. In fact, while agricultural microfirms are linked to seasonal productive cycles and take up long periods of time from seed to harvest – followed by transformation and commercialization of the products – many manufacturing microenterprises in labour intensive business are characterized for having much shorter productive schedules. Therefore, depending on the typology of the financed microenterprise, the financial exigencies MFIs have to fulfil are very different. Such elements significantly influence the products that MFIs provide as well as the duration of the microfinancing that has to be agreed.

More specifically, MFIs typically finance the working capital of beneficiaries, both in agricultural and manufacturing programmes. However, if considering agricultural enterprises, longer-term microcredits are necessary – providing eventually a grace period, to take into account the gap between beginning of production and commercialization – whereas shorter term microcredits with shorter repayment periods apply more often to manufacturing enterprises.

Less frequently, in addition to providing working capital, MFIs also provide the necessary resources to invest in fixed assets. The required financing in order to purchase or instal durable productive means is provided for single borrowers and, more often, for groups of beneficiaries – joint or independent – that share installations or machinery that are necessary for their own production processes. In such cases, despite the fact that the high value of the goods to be financed exceeds the traditional threshold of microfinance, the existence of a consortium of producers or of a homogeneous group of borrowers, which implies a joint obligation, allows such operations to be considered as part of microfinance activities.

3.4   Distinguishing features of microcredits

The term microcredit is used to identify a mixture of various financial and non-financial services. The different definitions adopted by the international organizations, as well as by practitioners and scholars, from time to time, emphasize different aspects raising doubts about what this term really means. The lack of an unequivocal categorization of microcredit creates certain difficulties, from the moment that it makes the MFIs' operating boundaries uncertain and complicates its

promotion and implementation within different regulatory structures. Regardless of the definitions preferred, the minimum distinctive elements that distinguish microcredit, in our opinion, refer to the following aspects:

- borrowers' target;
- clear prevalence of credit activity over other services;
- loan amount;
- repayment period;
- lack of usual collateral;

With reference to the *target beneficiaries*, alongside the principles described in section 3.2, as far as microcredit is concerned these must be people who have difficulty in accessing the traditional financial system, who have started or are about to start a business and need the financial resources that are necessary to carry out lasting investments, that is, the purchase of raw materials or goods in progress. In such context, therefore, the distinguishing element is represented by the presence of a microbusiness that is the main source of economical and financial support for the beneficiary and his family. On the other hand, the distribution of microloans to support consumption – although it could have the same technical and financial characteristics – does not fall within the realm of microcredit.

A second misinterpretation concerns the offer, alongside microcredit, of *non-financial services* that go beyond the supply of funds. The uncertainty derives from the fact that informal MFIs, which prioritize social objectives instead of sustainability, often offer, alongside credit services, technical support and training packages to the beneficiaries, in order to durably improve the technical skills and the productivity of the financed microbusinesses. In such cases, microcredit is considered to remain as such, also if it represents the minor part of a wider support and development cooperation project. However, if the credit activity is marginal in the project, the institutions that supply microloans cannot be considered in a strict sense as MFIs. Such a view, in the agreed operational contexts, has important consequences on the authorization and supervision profiles of the microfinance institutions, supporting the operations of smaller MFIs. On the other hand, in countries in which microfinance is more recent and the establishment of MFIs has benefited from more analytical and structured regulation bodies, credit operations that focus on the achievement of wider development projects are usually allowed only for formal and registered MFIs, which therefore are favoured.

A third distinguishing element of microcredit is the reduced single *amounts of the supplied loans*. The revolutionary principle of this financial approach is based on the fact that, by means of offering low-amount credit – which varies in different countries – it is possible to trigger a multiplying process that generates revenue. In general, the basic idea consists in the fact that microcredit also allows financially excluded people to start, or improve, production activities with higher return, up to the point where even the higher funding costs – compared with market conditions – can be compensated. Moreover, the effectiveness of microcredit is based on the fact that the offer of low-amount loans rescues the businesses from alternative financial circuits, such as usury; furthermore, it contributes to free microbusinesses from the excessive negotiating power of suppliers, that anticipate part of the inputs necessary to create the products and take away a significant part of the beneficiaries' margins.

The fourth distinctive feature of microcredit is the *short duration of the financing* and the high recovery rate of the supplied loans. The main working capital financing consists in the supply of short term loans, with a maturity usually below one year. Moreover, MFIs rarely supply credit lines to clients that have discretion in using them, preferring microcredits with predefined sinking plans and frequent instalments. The reason for having sinking plans with monthly, weekly or even daily instalments derives from the fact that many beneficiaries have never had any previous relationships with financial institutions and, therefore, are not used to longer-term cash flow managements. In addition, the choice of tightly scheduled repayment periods should be in line with the schedules of the commercialization of goods, which, in the case of the above-mentioned manufacturing micro-businesses, are very short, whereas for agricultural businesses there is usually a grace period during which, while waiting for the products to reach maturity, the borrower can freeze the payment of capital and interests.

The last distinguishing element of microcredit, regarding collateral policies, needs a specific closer examination that is described in the following section.

3.5   Collateral policies

The approaches used to draw up guarantees for the supplied microcredits probably represent the most innovating and original element of microcredit compared with traditional credit risk mitigation policies. The lack of traditional collateral, as well as of borrowers' certain, stable and documented revenues, has always represented the main limitation

to access formal credit for financially excluded customers and for poor people. Hence, the offer of microcredit has had to develop by using alternative forms of guarantee to traditional ones. On this matter, the pioneers of microfinance had the brilliant idea of developing and transforming into collateral all those intangible assets that the poorest people have: the sense of belonging to the same community and the reciprocal solidarity. Coherent with such an idea, the main risk mitigating methodologies used are *group lending* and *dynamic incentives*.

Group lending is the strategic choice of asking those who apply for a loan to search in their own community for other small producers, which need to be financed too, in order to create a group with them, and to ask the members of the group to enter a joint obligation. In case one affiliate of the group is unable to repay the instalments, the other members respond to its debts. Although there are different group lending approaches, in most cases the loan applicant, who does not have other guarantees, has to find a certain number of people – usually five – who also need microcredit and spontaneously decide to share the risk of other members of the same group that are unable to pay. Such searching is carried out by the potential borrowers in their community, in which there are people that trust one another. These links represent an important asset in certain contexts and are suitable for balancing the lack of usual collateral. The offer of microcredit to solidarity groups provides, first of all, that two members of the group receive the financing. If this is promptly repaid, after a few weeks two other members receive the loan; if they all keep repaying according to schedule, the person that formed the group also receives the microcredit.

The basic principle of group lending is called *peer monitoring*. The beneficiaries that belong to the same group carry out a constant mutual monitoring on the use of the received funds and on the repayment of capital and interests. In case one of the members is temporarily in economic difficulties, the architecture of group lending stimulates the members of the group to help the borrower to pay his debt; at the same time, peer monitoring creates social pressure, which is proportional to the intensity of the relationships between the members of the group, so that the borrower does his best to repay the loan. Since group lending and peer monitoring can only work in the presence of non-explicit inter-subjective bonds, such methodology is justly preferred in two contexts. First, group lending better applies to MFIs that offer low-amount microcredits. It is often verified that, as the single supplied amounts rise, resistance and mistrust towards joint obligations arises also among the members of the same community. Second, because that group lending is

based on the sense of belonging to the same community, this method-ology is more effective in social contexts in which such cohesion is stronger. In general, such contexts can be found in certain rural areas or, alternatively, in certain countries where the most disadvantaged part of society is less heterogeneous.

So far, group lending has represented the foundation of many micro-credit programmes. However, it does have its defects concerning the fact that the formation of solidarity groups leads to the same treatment towards all the members of the group; this can create problems such as *adverse selection* and *moral hazard*, because of the differences between the members of a group, in terms of risks concerning the borrowers themselves and their investments projects.

Dynamic incentives represent the second methodology of credit risk mitigation in microcredit. Since the demand for microcredit comes from subjects not used to dealing with financial institutions, a functional element in the establishment of a market discipline for beneficiaries could be represented by the fact that initially they could have access to a small loan; subsequently, if the loan is repaid in due time and, therefore, the beneficiary shows to have certain skills in cash flow management, he can ask for larger loans. Hence, by using dynamic incentives, MFIs limit the credit risk in the first phase and, at the same time, reduce the concentration of the loans portfolio. Meanwhile, borrowers start familiarizing with a scheduled financial commitment which, if honoured, represents a previous record for the assessment of the creditworthiness. In fact, it is necessary to remember that MFIs operate in contexts where historical records of loan applicants and public databases of their existing debits virtually do not exist.

Guarantees and financial innovation. Alongside the two methodologies mentioned above, it is possible to imagine more sophisticated and het-erogeneous approaches to reduce credit risk. Some of them have already been adopted by a certain number of MFIs; others may represent an ele-ment of inspiration for MFIs to achieve a more modern credit risk man-agement. Such approaches can be sorted, for expositive purposes, as product and process innovative orientations.

As for *innovative products*, regarding credit risk mitigation it is worth mentioning *compulsory savings* and the establishment of *guarantee funds*. With the first MFIs can ask the beneficiaries to use a percentage of the supplied microcredits as compulsory savings, in order to reduce the bor-rower's exposure in case of default. Instead, guarantee funds are finan-cial resources put aside in order to cover the risk that some borrowers will not repay the capital and the interests. In case of default of the

beneficiary, the guarantee fund is used partially or totally to repay the remaining debt. Such funds can be established by the MFIs by putting aside a percentage of the interests earned from the supplied loans, or by local bodies or institutions operating in the development of the area, which collaborate in microfinance projects as guarantors. On the other hand, *process innovation* leads to innovative financial structures for microfinance. These are split into two main typologies: the first consists in the creation of a special purpose vehicle (SPV); the second provides a direct financing for the beneficiary using a typical scheme of assets segregated for a business. Both structures are used when there is a large number of beneficiaries organised in associations or cooperatives.

In the first option the isolation of the project risk is achieved by using an SPV, which becomes the central point of the contractual network of the whole programme (Figure 3.1). More specifically, this structure provides that a financial intermediary (sponsor), together with the project's promoting institution (promoter), sets up a Special Purpose Vehicle (SPV), purposely designed for the single project. The sponsor, which holds 100 per cent of SPV's capital, provides the vehicle with a fund that is only used for the achievement of the microcredit programme. The promoter, which can be an NGO or a local development institution, carries out the management and the administration of the fund and the control on the performance of the activities. Generally, unless the sponsor has a local network, or the promoter is certified to perform credit activities, the supply of credit to the beneficiaries is carried out by a third-party bank. In order to do this, the promoter will open a deposit in this bank using

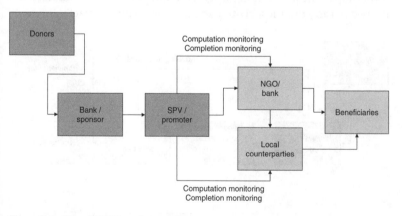

Figure 3.1   Use of SPV in microcredit
Source: La Torre and Vento (2005).

the funds provided by the sponsor. The sponsor remains the only holder of the fund and of the profits that may derive from the use of the amounts. The microcredits granted to the beneficiaries must be used to support the programme's activities and to purchase the goods necessary to carry out the activities. The profits deriving from the activities must be used by the beneficiaries to repay the received loans; the repayment of the capital and the interests to the financing body has priority on all the other costs concerning the activities of the promoter and of the depositing bank. As a guarantee on its investment, the financing institution can also use the goods purchased by the beneficiaries for their activities: in fact, such goods are part of the SPV's assets from the moment they have been purchased. The promoter is responsible of the project's achievement and of the regularity and transparency of the funds' administration. So, the credit risk management is carried out both by using a SPV, in order to isolate the project risk from the risks of the beneficiaries' and promoter's activities, and by having guarantees on the final products and on the goods purchased by the beneficiaries. Moreover, such structures always include a *computation* activity carried out by the sponsor, which allows them to have a constant control of the financial flow, by also using the information provided by the promoter.

A second structural option isolates the project risk without using an SPV. In this case, there is a tight link between the granted financing and the project to be achieved (Figure 3.2). The specific national regulations allow such a scheme under different legal patterns; besides the possible contextual legal backgrounds, the aim is to guarantee for the financing bank the ownership of the project and the legal certainty that the lent amounts will be used to carry out the activities set in the financing contract.

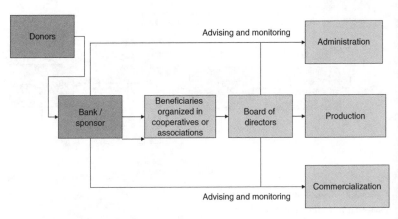

Figure 3.2   Use of segregated assets in microcredit
Source: La Torre and Vento (2005)

Such structure, generally used to finance cooperatives operating in many different sectors, which includes a direct relationship between the sponsor and the beneficiary and cannot count on the monitoring activities carried out by the promoter, adopts alternative instruments of credit risk management. Alongside the asset separation of the assigned fund, the financing bank adds the application of certain *covenants*, which are compulsory for the beneficiary and can be applied to the production phase as well as to the commercialization phase. As it is generally made for cooperatives that carry out many diversified activities compared with those stated in the contract, this structure provides that the sponsor must carry out a number of activities finalized to guarantee a correct administration, an appreciable level of accounting separation between the different activities and an accurate commercial plan specifically adapted to the financed project. For such reasons, activities of *administrative monitoring, technical monitoring* and *marketing assistance* are always carried out by the financing bank. So, compared with a financial architecture based on the SPV and on the technical and *administrative monitoring, technical monitoring* and *marketing assistance* are always carried out by the financing bank. Thus, compared with a financial architecture based on the SPV and on the technical and administrative support provided by the promoter, this structure requires a more invasive attitude of the sponsor in the beneficiary's working context, which means the use of specific covenants in the technical-administrative monitoring and in the commercial support (Table 3.1).

Table 3.1 Main credit risk mitigation strategies

	Strategies	Main features
1	Group lending	• peer monitoring • it works properly as long as the bonds in the community are strong • equal treatment to different borrowers, which can determine adverse selection and moral hazard
2	Dynamic incentives	• increase the amount of loans through time • useful to get the borrowers used to dealing with financial intermediaries • they reduce portfolio concentration
3	Other guarantees deriving from financial innovation	• compulsory savings to reduce exposure • guarantee funds to partially transfer on other subjects the default risk of the borrowers • special purpose vehicles and segregated capital used to isolate the project risk

3.6 Interest rates in microcredit

Among the many distinguishing features of microcredit, compared with traditional credit, the interest rate policies are described independently. These represent one of the most controversial and discussed aspects of microfinance. In fact, in the literature and among practitioners there is a contrast between those who think that, since microcredit is offered to disadvantaged subjects, it should be supplied at more favourable conditions than traditional credit, and those who claim that the beneficiaries of microcredit projects are not interest-rate sensitive, because the benefit of having access to credit is higher than the cost of financing, also when interest rates are higher than market rates. Besides, ethical and management considerations,[4] in terms of pricing it is not possible to determine, in abstract, an ideal level of interest rates for microcredit. It depends on many factors, of which only some are controlled by MFIs. However, it is necessary to identify the variables that have to be considered for a correct determination of rates, taking into account that the revenue equilibrium of an MFI is determined when:

costs + mark up = interests + fees

Loan pricing in microcredit has to be fixed coherently with the cost structure of MFIs. Accordingly, costs can be split into:

- Funding costs
- Operating costs
- Loan loss and currency risk provision
- Cost of capital, including inflation

Alongside the costs listed above, it is necessary to add a high or low risk premium, according to the type of institution and to the market in which they operate, which must be paid for the business risk of MFIs. Any determination of the rate policies that ignores just one of the above-mentioned elements determines, in the absence of stable and durable external subsidies, conditions of operational non-sustainability in the medium and long term.[5]

Regardless of inflation and capital cost, which depends on the MFIs' nature and origin of funds, it is necessary to make some considerations regarding the first three cost subcategories listed above. *Funding costs* mainly depend on the financing sources of MFIs; it is possible to identify three main sources. First, MFIs can aim to attract grants and soft

loans from donors by proposing some projects to them. On the other hand, these institutions can get into debt with financial intermediaries, which act like first level banks. Finally, they can collect public deposits, but only in countries and operational contexts where it is permitted.

The different funding strategies are not indifferent to collection stability and to costs. In fact, the collection of subsidized funds has low costs, sometimes no costs at all, but is very unstable, since donors' financing priorities can change over time. The collection of financing from financial institutions, including development multilateral banks and local development agencies, is characterized by having considerable costs and implies more or less influence on the strategies of MFIs. Finally, the collection of public deposits presents lower costs and higher stability, as long as MFIs are able to achieve a significant minimum volume of savings, and determine a higher management responsibility for the MFI, which has to comply with stricter supervision obligations. Consequently, a funding diversification strategy, also including public savings, is rewarding for the MFIs' management. Such an approach, however, cannot be pursued by all MFIs; in particular, the combined activities of savings collection and credit granting need an organizational structure and an internal auditing system that only larger institutions are able to set up. On the other hand, the collection of public deposits implies some risks that the depositors themselves are not always able to understand or adequately price; for such purpose there are authorization and prudential supervision schemes that limit, and sometimes stop, MFIs' collections.

Operating costs represent the highest costs for MFIs. The activity of MFIs, in fact, differs from traditional credit intermediaries because it is based on a closer and better mutual acquaintance between credit officers and beneficiaries. The fact that the distributing structure is based on a network of credit officers who visit the clients frequently, implies a higher level of operating costs. Moreover, the reduced average amount of the supplied microcredits does not always allow for the fixed management costs of the single microloans to be adequately shared. Therefore, such costs represent the most significant element in determining the rates of the microcredits.

Finally, the third type of cost that influences the determination of the interest rates is the *loan loss provision*. Having said that the quality of MFIs' credit portfolio is often better than that of the traditional intermediaries operating in the same geographical areas, these depend, first of all, on the ability of MFIs to carry out an adequate screening and monitoring of the borrowers. Besides the ability of MFIs to select clients,

Table 3.2 Three main elements in interest rates determination

	Elements	Main drivers
1	Funding costs	• Capability to attract subsidized funds • Cost of funding versus other financial inter-mediaries and/or institutions • Capability to collect deposits from public
2	Operating costs	• Net of credit officers • Average dimension of microloans
3	Loan loss provisions	• Capability to screen and monitor borrowers • Recovery management procedures

---

Box 3.1 Calculating interest rates

Interest on a microcredit can be calculated according to several methods. Here, we focus our attention on the two most common: the *declining balance method* and the *flat method*.

In the *declining balance method* interest rates are computed as a percentage of the amount outstanding over the loan term. Therefore, the borrower pays interest on the principal that he still owes. The payment made each period is constant, whereas the principal increases over time and the interest decreases.

In the *flat method* interest is computed as a percentage of the initial micro-credit rather than the amount outstanding, which is declining over time. Thus, interest is always computed on the initial amount disbursed. In this case payments, principal and interest are constant over time.

By using the flat method the actual amount of interest charged is much higher than in declining balance method. Declining balance method, however, seems to be the most suitable method of interest computation, because it calculates interest only on the amount actually due, and not also on the percentage of principal already repaid.

---

the volume of credit losses are influenced by the decisions regarding the area in which they should operate, by the sector that should be financed and by the management of insolvencies, when the borrowers are clearly unable to repay the received microloans (Table 3.2).

In order that an MFI can reach the different levels of sustainability described in Chapter 4, it is necessary that the costs listed above are taken into consideration when determining interest rates and fees. However, this doesn't mean that the above-mentioned cost elements have to be completely transferred on to the borrowers, since many MFIs are able to operate in conditions of sustainability thanks to the external contribution of grants and soft loans. Yet, it is important that every MFI is constantly aware of what its economic-financial performance would

be without subsidized funds, in order to avoid misunderstandings on the different levels of sustainability in which it would operate without the subsidies.

Finally, in order adequately to evaluate the interest flow against the cost elements listed above, it is also important to define carefully the interest calculation methods used by MFIs. The use of certain methodologies rather than others provides very different cash flows, especially in operational contexts that are characterized by very a high interest rate level. Box 3.1 describes the two main interest calculation methods that are more often used in microfinance.

3.7 Conclusion

Microcredit is now almost unanimously considered as a financial technique that, since it needs a very modest volume of resources, is able to contribute in a significant way to the development of those economic activities that benefit from it. The key of such success mostly depends on its main technical features. Therefore, microcredit shows its maximum effectiveness in those cases where the beneficiaries have adequate technical skills in the production of marketable goods and services, but lack of the financial means for their commercialization and distribution. Regarding the offer of microcredits, these usually have higher recovery rates compared with traditional intermediaries. The reason for such success predominantly derives from the typical technicalities of microcredit. These are conceived in order to enhance a combination of specific features of the borrowers, which, in a microcredit mechanism, can represent intangible assets. In the same way, the guarantee policy within the offer of microcredit is conceived in order to reduce the risk of exposure by applying concepts that are fairly distant from the culture of traditional financial intermediaries, such as peer monitoring or social pressure for the repayment of loans, but also by using more sophisticated financial structures that, with the necessary expedients, can be usefully applied to MFIs.

One of the central and most discussed elements in the offer of microcredit concerns the determination of the level of interest rates. Whatever the mission of the MFIs is, the definition of the rates must take into account all the costs that the institutions have to face, in order to avoid supplying loans at unsustainable conditions.

4
Sustainability and Outreach: the Goals of Microfinance

Gianfranco Vento

4.1 Introduction

The financial sustainability of microfinance projects and institutions consists mainly in finding a balance between the profit gained from the projects and the cost of carrying them out. This variable is taken into great consideration by MFIs, donors and investors who bring financial support to microfinance and the various stakeholders. In pursuing the goal of sustainability the conditions are created so that the results obtained may continue over time and, ultimately, so that the initiatives and institutions are self-sufficient from outside contributions. The sustainability of microfinance programmes is traditionally related to the social benefit that derives from them, usually meant, though not exclusively, as the ability to reach the poorest sector of the population. Such concept of 'depth' of intervention is called *outreach* in specialist terminology.

The balance between lasting sustainability of microfinance projects and institutions, and the choice of beneficiaries and the products and services to offer, represents one of the most widely discussed dilemmas among microfinance academics and practitioners. This chapter will discuss, first, the definitions of sustainability and outreach, identifying the various meanings of these broad concepts. Then, with regard to the trade-off between sustainability and outreach, the main criteria to be considered when selecting beneficiaries will be outlined. The aim is to clarify whether, and in what way, working with especially poor customers could affect the offer of financial services in terms of sustainability. Finally, this chapter will propose a range of operating and management choices suitable for reconciling the aims of sustainability with those of outreach.

4.2 Sustainability and outreach

In microfinance, sustainability is understood primarily as the ability of MFIs to repeat loans over time (*substantial financial sustainability*), regardless of how the financial stability of the project or institution is achieved. Substantial financial sustainability (Figure 4.1) describes the ability to cover the costs necessary for the start-up and management of the microfinance activity, whether through the profits from services offered, in particular financial ones, or through grants and soft loans. In a stricter sense, therefore, to be financially sustainable a project or institution must receive a flow of donations and profits, from interest and commission, that cover operating costs, inflation costs, costs related to the portfolio devaluation, financial costs, a risk premium and the return on capital brought by project investors or MFI shareholders (Figure 4.2).

The entry of private investors into the microfinance market, as well as the increasing scarcity of public funds, has brought *financial self-sustainability* to the attention of donors and practitioners in recent years. This should not be confused with substantial financial sustainability. When we refer to substantial financial sustainability, grants and subsidized funds are also included among the items that contribute to cover costs and to stabilize the income of an MFI; whereas, with financial

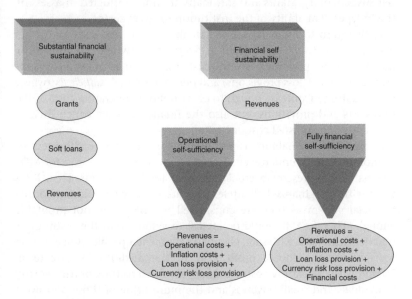

Figure 4.1   Different levels of microfinance sustainability

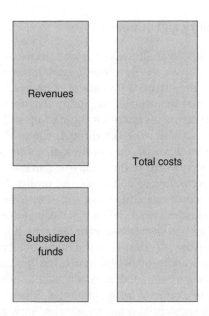

Figure 4.2   Substantial financial sustainability

self-sustainability, grants and soft loans are not considered in assessing the independent ability of the institution to cover costs.

With regard to financial self-sustainability, it is necessary to further distinguish between *operational self-sufficiency* (where the operating income covers operating costs, the cost of inflation, loan loss provisions and currency risk loss provisions) and *fully financial self-sufficiency* (where the operating income is enough to cover not only operating costs, inflation costs and provisions, but also the financing costs, which include debt costs and adjusted cost of capital).

Analysing sustainability is important for any type of business or economic activity undertaken. However, in microfinance and for MFIs especially, it represents a crucial element for two reasons. First, MFIs work with marginalized clientele, who are not accepted in the formal financial system as they are considered too risky and not profitable enough. Therefore, it would be logical to assume that the institutions that decide to work with such clientele have greater problems in covering costs with an adequate profit flow in the medium to long term. Secondly, the operating costs necessary for the screening of trustworthy individuals and small business and the monitoring of those borrowers are such that, when compared to the profit made from a single client,

they could show little advantage in working for such small amounts. However, a project or an institution may be substantially financially sustainable in that it is able to attract a constant flow of subsidized funds over time, which significantly reduces financial costs and allows the profits to cover residual costs, but not financially self-sustainable since, because of the lack of subsidies and therefore funded at market costs, it would be unable to achieve profit stability.

It follows that, in analysing sustainability and in distinguishing between substantial sustainability and self-sustainability, a central role is played by subsidies, from which, in different ways, the vast majority of microfinance programmes and MFIs have benefited. In fact, although the goal of leaving aside the donors' funds has been considered by many lecturers as an essential step in order to make microfinance a stable instrument to sustain the poorest people, as well as those financially excluded, there are few cases of microfinance institutions or programmes which, in some form, have never received subsidies and are in a condition of economic stability.

Subsidies may be present in various forms and at different stages of the project. With regard to typology, subsidies can be divided into *grants*, soft debts and *discounts on expenses*. Grants consist mainly of public and private direct donations (direct equity grants or direct profit grants, depending on the accountancy policy of the MFIs) and in paid-in capital (so called 'in-kinds', such as the offer of instrumental goods needed for an adequate performance, the offer of technical services and training, as well as of management and administration consulting services). With regard to timing, MFIs can receive subsidies both during the start-up phase, when the costs necessary to set up the activity are far greater than the profits, as well as at later stages.

The search for a balance between costs and profits in the running of MFIs brings us back to the debate in the literature about the precise nature of microfinance. In this regard, there are two opposing theories: *Financial Service Approach* and *Poverty Lending Approach*. In the first approach microfinance is considered as a further division of the financial services market, with the aim of reaching financially excluded individuals who have limited access to the formal financial system. For others, microfinance is above all a tool of international cooperation, which should support the funding of economic initiatives at less demanding conditions than those of the market, assuming that financial inclusion generates important positive externalities, beyond purely economic features. The debate, triggered by these two positions, points out the need for microfinance practitioners to adopt operating approaches that correspond to the

planned objectives. The Poverty Lending Approach tends to help a smaller number of people over a shorter time, providing only basic services. In contrast the Self Sustainability Approach provides support policies for financially excluded people by increasing the number of beneficiaries and the services supply period.

Thus, it is important to examine more closely the type of aims and benefits that should inspire microfinance programmes that are addressed towards outreach. Although the literature offers various taxonomies of the values that express outreach, it is possible to define the concept in two partially opposing ways: *depth* and *breadth* (Figure 4.3). Depth represents the poverty level of the beneficiaries involved, whereas breadth concerns the number of clients reached. In the first case, in terms of overall benefit, outreach towards poorer beneficiaries is preferred despite the total number of potential customers. Assuming that in social welfare the community prioritizes the poorest individuals, the depth of a microfinance involvement is proportional to the net benefit that derives from the offer of financial services to those people. The basic idea is that the benefit of receiving a loan for the poorest individuals is greater than for people at higher social level. On the other hand, priority to breadth implies a preference towards a wider consideration of customers, although they are not all categorized as 'the poorest of the poor'. In a context in which the demand for financial services from the poorest and the financially excluded people is higher than the supply, the ability to reach a larger number of beneficiaries becomes a goal itself.

In literature, other aspects of outreach are often mentioned, which however are referable to simple proxies of breadth and depth. An important initial indicator of the depth of the programme is the loan amount, since most financially excluded clients tend to ask for smaller loans. Furthermore, outreach can be considered as *worth to clients*, that is, an indication of the client's attitude towards paying for services, since these

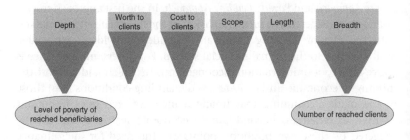

Figure 4.3   Dimensions of microfinance outreach

significantly meet their own financial needs. It indicates the maximum amount that the borrower would reach in order to obtain a loan. A poorer beneficiary obviously accepts to pay more. A greater *worth to client* may correspond to greater depth.

The third variable of outreach is the *cost to clients* for the financial services achieved. This represents the cost of the loan for the debtor. It is the sum of direct cash payments for interest and fees, plus transaction costs. Generally, the cost to client is positively related to depth, because, in theory, greater depth implies riskier clients, as well as fixed operating costs shared by a smaller number of beneficiaries. The fourth proxy of outreach is *scope*, that is, the number of typologies of financial contracts supplied by MFIs, and the fifth regards the length of the microfinance programme: this represents the period of time during which microfinance services are offered. An indirect proxy of length is the obtainment of profits that guarantee the carrying out of the programmes, even without lasting donations. The underlying idea is that the offer of microfinance should not run out in a short space of time. Consequently it is assumed that the offer is positively correlated to profits generated by MFIs, since the profits making can represent a valid proxy by the fact that the MFIs continue their activity over time. The greater the variety of the offered products and financial services, the greater the length of operations and, presumably, the greater the outreach. Scope and length, however, can be associated to programmes that prioritize depth as well as those that focus on breadth.

4.3 Sustainability: how to reach it

Within the debate regarding the sustainability of microfinance institutions and programmes, it is possible to identify different levels of sustainability which increases proportionally to the independence of programmes and MFIs from grants and soft loans. The aim of sustainability assumes greater importance when referring to MFIs. The basic idea, in order to affirm that an MFI is sustainable, is that the operative return is sufficient to cover the institution's costs. Thus, the different attitudes to being sustainable depends on the specific relevance of assets and liabilities.

In a traditional microfinance institution, return consists in the interests earned from loans and in the commissions obtained from other services. The return flow depends mainly on the size of the loans portfolio, on the ability and will of individuals to repay and on the breadth of the range of services offered. Hence, concerning return, the key variables are referred to a few balance-sheet items, which can be significantly

influenced by the strategic goals of MFIs regarding marketing. As far as costs go, the analysis of the variables that influence sustainability are much more complex. In breaking up the typical costs of a microfinance institution it is possible to identify at least four distinct categories:

- *operating costs*, necessary for the activities of the microfinance institution and the performance of the core business. These include also the amortization quotes of pluri-annual factors of production used in the productive process;
- *inflation costs*, which reduce over time the real value of the funds that MFIs use to supply credit;
- *loan losses provisions* and *currency risk loss provisions* to be used for covering expected losses;
- *financial costs*, which are paid to those who provide funds to the MFI as debts or equity.

According to the balance-sheet structure, and to its impact on sustainability, it is possible to divide MFIs into four categories (Figure 4.4). The first level of MFIs, which depend on grants and soft loans comprises all the institutions for which the revenues from interest and commission on the products and services offered are not sufficient to cover the costs of the funds used in intermediation. These are normally informal or semi-formal MFIs, mainly small NGOs, who are financed by donations and

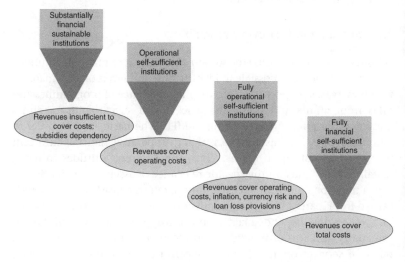

Figure 4.4   Four degrees of sustainability for MFIs

supply microcredits to very poor customers at interest rates lower than the market rates. For these institutions, therefore, the substantial financial sustainability is only guaranteed by the subsidies they obtain from donors and from those who consider it valuable to invest in microfinance (*subsidies dependency*).

The second level of sustainability is represented by the institutions that are able to achieve a revenue flow that covers the operating costs deriving from their activities (*operational self-sufficiency*). These are semi-formal MFIs that can diversify the source of funding in order not to depend entirely on donors' funds. They also offer interest rates on microcredits that are lower than the market rates, but higher than those of first-level MFIs. These MFIs pay greater attention to the market and to commercial policies. However, they do not have a revenue flow that allows them to compensate inflation costs, to save sufficient resources to face loan and currency losses provisions and to cover their financial costs.

The third level of sustainability applies to the MFIs that are able to generate enough revenues to cover inflation costs, credit and currency losses, as well as operating costs (*fully operational self-sufficiency*). These are usually formal MFIs that, on the one hand, are capable of significantly diversifying funding policies, to the point of collecting deposits from customers, and, on the other, able to standardize the supply and monitoring processes on microcredits, allowing them to minimize operational costs. Such institutions, often legally operating as microfinance banks or as specialized divisions of commercial banks, apply interest rates on their loans roughly corresponding to the conditions applied to ordinary banks' customers. However, these institutions still partially depend on third-party funds – to a greater or lesser degree according to the circumstances – which help to reduce the otherwise unsustainable financial costs. These funds are normally provided to MFIs by the recourse to soft loans or other grants supplied by international donors.

The highest level of sustainability (*fully financial self-sufficiency*) is that of formal MFIs that succeed in covering all costs, including financial costs at market rates, with their revenues. Only a small number of MFIs, mainly formal MFIs, have actually achieved this level of financial independence. Being a fully self-sufficient institution is a prerequisite for MFIs to be able to repay the capital provided by shareholders. These institutions normally collect a large percentage of funds received from depositors and use them for loans priced at higher interest rates than those offered to traditional customers, owing to the scarce interest rate elasticity of the market demand. Besides, a small number of more efficient MFIs are able to reduce the cost to user by exploiting cross subsidiarization

with other businesses. This is a more practical solution for those MFIs that are part of financial groups or are linked by equity participation to banks and other financial intermediaries.

One indicator that can be used to measure the MFIs' sustainability dependence from external support, and to include the institution in one of the above-mentioned categories, is the Subsidy Dependence Index (SDI). This index, produced by Jacob Yaron (1992), gives us information on the level of interest rates needed for microloans in order to operate without subsidies. The value of interest rate r^*, which determines the balance between the costs and revenues of a MFI, can be found by solving the following equation:[1]

$$L (1+r^*)(1-d) = L+C+S \qquad (4.1)$$

where L is the amount of loans not in default, $(1-d)$ is the percentage of loan portfolio estimated to be repaid, C represents the total costs (including the cost of capital) and S indicates the subsidies received by the MFI. Evidencing interest rates, we get:

$$r^* = [C+S+dL]/[L(1-d)] \qquad (4.2)$$

In most operating contexts such interest rate would largely be higher than market rates. In reality, as previously stated, the cases of MFIs offering microcredits at interest rates that meet the SDI are very rare. This implies that a strict application of the SDI should be considered as an extreme limit, theoretically, in an approach towards maximizing sustainability without considering social aims.

4.4 Outreach: how to select the beneficiaries

As previously highlighted regarding sustainability, outreach – intended as the depth of distribution and commercial policies – is an aspect that does not only concern MFIs. Decisions regarding the selection of target customers, and the operating strategies to match products and services to various segments of customers represent some of the fundamental elements of the strategic planning process of financial intermediaries. Decisions on outreach, however, are crucial factors in microfinance, in identifying the beneficiaries who should be selected in order to maximize the social impact of the initiatives undertaken. Aside from the ability to repay loans – which can be considered as a proxy of sustainability – it is important for MFIs to understand if there are some common features of

the beneficiaries that are highly significant in order to improve the social impact of microfinance programmes or to increase the sustainability, with the social impact being constant.

The aspects of outreach described above, and the related proxies, cannot be used as operating instruments in every context for three main reasons. First, variables such as depth, social value or worth to user are difficult to measure by objective criteria and thus cannot be compared over space and time. Furthermore, the different subcategories of outreach have a high level of internal idiosyncrasy, in the sense that greater attention to the depth of the programmes, which induces an MFI to work with the poorest of the poor in a given region, may go against the goals of breadth concerning the number of beneficiaries. Finally, some elements of outreach, such as the comparison between the costs and social benefits of microfinance, covered by the concept of breadth, have an evident macroeconomic nature. Therefore, it is not easy to determine the impact a microfinance initiative might have, as well as the necessary time in order to have the desired effect on the involved communities.

Consequently, considering that, at present, the demand for financial services from financially excluded individuals greatly exceeds the supply, both in developing countries and in more developed ones, it is important to identify other variables that can be considered during the beneficiaries' selection process.

A key variable that often determines the success of a microfinance programme is whether the beneficiaries possess *good operating skills* in the field of activity where they work or intend to work. Typical clients of MFIs, which have a greater level of sustainability, can be distinguished by their significant knowledge and experience of the technical operational procedures needed to create products and services, as well as by their capability in the marketing of those products. Nevertheless, these microentrepreneurs experience a structural lack of financial resources, partly due to the low self-financing capability, since financially excluded individuals, both in developing countries as well as in industrialized ones, address almost all their income to consumption. Consequently, for such typology of customers, the role of MFIs is to offer microcredits, and occasionally other financial services, to be used for the funding of working capital, and more rarely of intangible assets that are needed in the production process.

Another common feature of the good outcome of numerous microfinance initiatives and institutions, is the choice of *working with women*, earmarking a significant percentage of loans portfolio to them. In fact, regardless of geographic area and social–economic background, women

have shown they are more careful in using the supplied loans for small businesses, or simply for self-employment, as well as more punctual in loans repayment. The main reason for a greater number of microfinance programmes aimed at women is that women are more cautious in their investment choices and are more sensitive to social pressure within peer groups. Moreover, women are poorer than men. Finally, it is believed that, other factors being constant, the social and economic impact of providing microloans for women is greater than for men, also in terms of increased empowerment, due to unequal opportunities regarding the female population.

4.5   The microfinance dilemma: sustainability vs outreach

As stated in the previous sections, sustainability of microfinance institutions represents the essential prerequisite for MFIs to be able to continue to provide their services in the medium and long term, as any other firm. On the other hand, in cases of financial exclusion – in which the demand for financial services from disadvantaged individuals greatly exceeds the supply – an analysis concerning outreach is necessary in order to address the resources, which are by definition scarce, towards financing productive microactivities that are able to provide the highest return.

In literature, and among practitioners, sustainability and outreach have been deepened in order to verify the existence of a trade-off between the objectives of economic and financial equilibrium and the social goals.[2] Considerations concerning a preference towards providing stronger support to depth goals rather than breadth goals are typical dilemmas in welfare economy, which are difficult to be dealt with without an exhaustive analysis of the context. Furthermore, it is common to find an orientation in literature aiming to stress the need to carry out corner choices between sustainability objectives and outreach objectives. Hence, this chapter avoids revisiting the historical debate regarding the priority to be assigned to different models of outreach and their compatibility with sustainability. Instead, it is more useful to examine the aspects of management which allow for finding a better equilibrium between sustainability and outreach.

The dimensions of outreach must be taken into account by those who intend to put together a microfinance programme but should be evaluated in the context of single programmes or the medium- and long-term strategies of MFIs. According to MFIs' codes of conduct, the different

aspects of outreach can have different relevance, by rising, dropping or even being cancelled.

Pricing policies adopted by MFIs show the dichotomy between sustainability and outreach. When, for example, an institution decides to improve sustainability, by raising the clients' commissions, there is the risk of not reaching all potential beneficiaries with the service; consequently, the value of breadth goes down, whereas the value of depth increases. In this case, the cost to user increases because the increase in operational costs is transferred to the customers. When an MFI decides to keep the cost to user low, this means a decrease in operating margins and consequently in length – and ultimately in sustainability. If an MFI fixes high interest rates to cover operating and funding costs, both the depth and breadth risk are affected. In this case, applying interest rates higher than the market can be justified by the fact that, for financed individuals, the financial costs are totally compensated by the benefits deriving from access to the credit.

If, instead, an MFI, in trying to keep interest rates on credit low for outreach purposes, cannot achieve full sustainability, it is likely to create some distorting effects. In fact, first, the offer of financial services, especially microcredits at lower interest rates than the market distorts the competition between those financed by MFIs who take this approach and the microenterprises that are financed in market conditions. Moreover, the fact of not achieving full sustainability leads over time some MFIs to leave the market, which can cause serious problems for the clients who had deposited savings with them but also for the microenterprises that lose their main source of funding.

However, it is useful to underline how for some categories of beneficiaries the dichotomy between sustainability and outreach is less important. In fact, non-bankable individuals who are able to create products and services that can be placed on the market are able to obtain margins for which the difference between the cost of funding, available at market rates, and the higher one actually obtained from the MFIs, does not have a significant effect. In this way, supposing that the microcredit beneficiary – being a small producer by definition and, therefore, unable to shift the supply curve, as a price taker – has the productive capabilities to achieve significant margins, he will be able to pay higher interest rates during the period in which he will continue to be considered unbankable, and at the same time he will remain in economic equilibrium. If, however, the spread between the market rate and that applied by MFIs could jeopardize the profitability, and therefore the sustainability of the funded microenterprise, it is unadvisable

to proceed with the funding both in the interest of the beneficiary and also of the MFI.

4.6 The policies for improving sustainability

In analysing the problems of MFI sustainability in management terms, the balance between revenues and costs in offering microfinance services can be seen as a matter of analysis and improvement of the performance over time.

Portfolio management

With regard to profits, the main source of income for MFIs, and in some cases the only one, is the interest from loans portfolio and the related commission. However, it is vital for MFIs' stability that they maintain a high quality of credit portfolio and an adequate credit risk management, in order to minimize loan losses.[3] The average quality of MFIs' loans portfolio is, in many cases, higher than that of formal financial intermediaries working in the same context. These elements, besides shattering the myth that less wealthy borrowers are not good clients, highlight a better credit selection process and a subsequent better monitoring by MFIs, compared with traditional intermediaries, which should be better recognized.

As far as the selection process is concerned, the elements that seem to affect the quality of the portfolio the most can be identified in the proximity and the deep acquaintance between the MFIs' credit officers and the funded borrowers, in the use of specific technicalities conceived for microfinance – such as peer monitoring, dynamic incentives, etc. – and in the decision to lend to customers who have technical and operating skills but lack of funds. Instead, the quality of monitoring on the financed borrowers significantly depends on the ability and reliability of the credit officers, on the existence of at least two levels of control and, more generally, on the analysis and standardization of processes, which even smaller MFIs must somehow formalize. Furthermore, monitoring is made more efficient and timely by technological development, which allows MFIs to process a significant amount of data in less time and at a lower cost, like traditional intermediaries.[4] The considerations made above do not rule out the possibility that MFIs should further improve credit management and operational procedures. Chapters 5 and 6 cover the possible methodologies for better risks and processes management in detail. Thus, the contribution that banks and traditional financial intermediaries can offer to MFIs may have great importance: the use of

risk measurement and management models used by banks and the outsourcing of some phases of the production process may, in fact, be the key to a more efficient management.

Pricing policy

The amount of interest earned is also a function of the interest rates fixed by MFIs. Interest rate policies are one of the most disputed topics in microfinance. In defining interest rates and commissions, MFIs cannot neglect the need to cover the costs of funding, the operational costs to be spread on each loan, the devaluation of purchasing power of currency due to inflation, loan loss and currency loss provisions and a risk premium to remunerate the business risk.

In addition, the process of fixing interest rates must also consider further four factors. First, MFIs must consider the pricing policies adopted by other intermediaries, formal and non-formal, operating in the same context, in order to avoid offering products too far off market conditions, and thus risking not meeting demand. Second, like practices in use in traditional intermediaries, interest rate policies should reflect the higher or lower recovery rate implicit in the different technical lending products, considering the existence of collateral or other factors that may determine a pre-emption right for MFIs in case of default by the borrower. Furthermore, the fixing of interest rates cannot avoid considerations regarding triggering adverse selection and moral hazard processes, where interest rates levels are considered too high by the borrowers. Finally, the experience of many microfinance programmes carried out at particularly favourable interest rates have shown how such programmes attract different individuals from the original beneficiaries to apply for a loan; this leads to very modest performance levels for MFIs.

Therefore, to achieve pricing that meets sustainability objectives, MFIs must consider both internal management variables and external market variables. However, it is also true that a greater efficiency in the credit process and in the measuring of credit risk by MFIs could contribute to reducing the cost to user, other conditions being constant, without compromising sustainability. Also in this case, collaboration with traditional financial intermediaries could help MFIs in such strategic activities.

Efficiency

On the cost front, the situation seems equally critical, since it is affected by the contexts in which the different MFIs decide to work. As far as financial costs are concerned, the vast majority of MFIs, as previously mentioned, are highly dependent on external funds, in the form of subsidies. These

funds have very low or no costs but are somehow unstable and uncertain over time, depending on donors' evaluations on which MFIs have no influence. Therefore, obtaining subsidies is not necessarily a negative factor in itself; it is actually useful for sustainability. What is worrying is the unpredictability of these subsidies. Thus, the efficiency of an MFI should not be measured so much on a lower dependence on grants and loans, but on the capability of keeping these funding sources stable over time. This capability represents an intangible asset for MFIs that allows for a lower cost to user and facilitates the goal of sustainability. Moreover, given that most of the MFIs that are not self-sustainable receive external subsidies, a deeper analysis of the optimization of subsidies is necessary. In this regard it is believed subsidies should mainly be finalized to finance the start-up phases of MFIs, bridging the gap between revenues, which at the start-up stage are usually not enough, and costs. Vice versa, if subsidies were used by MFIs to keep the intermediation costs low, the effect of this policy would be to distort allocation processes, to alter market competition, and probably to worsen the portfolio quality in the long run.

In the same way, the capability of differentiating sources of funding should be evaluated. Many MFIs, with the aim of reducing their dependence on external funds, have for a long time extended their activity in collecting savings from the public. In fact, numerous MFIs have shown in practice how even the poorest individuals have a savings capability, often not held in monetary form. Such savings, if reintroduced in the financial system, could usefully contribute to funding investment projects. The collection of deposits by MFIs, however, is not always permitted by prudential regulations, and, nevertheless, it exposes the depositor to the risks deriving from the misuse of funds by MFIs in excessively risky business, triggering agency problems. Finally, the reduction of funding costs can also be achieved through recourse to types of collection related to ethical finance, not greatly exploited so far by MFIs, with particular reference to the collection of Ethical Investment Funds and Ethical Pension Funds.

The second variable affecting the efficiency of MFIs and their capability to exist is their ability to keep operational costs low. Managing numerous microloans having a small single amount, as usual in microcredit, as well as the high frequency repayments of loan instalments, entails a significantly high level of operational costs, mainly due to personnel costs. The main effort of the most sustainable MFIs, therefore, is focused once again on the standardization of procedures, without transforming the universally acknowledged strong points of microfinance, such as close

contact and deep mutual acquaintance between institutions and beneficiaries. Even in this sphere, interaction with financial intermediaries can be the key to success.

The factors discussed do not cover the full panorama of policies towards improving sustainability. The solutions offered by the market for sustainable outreach are many and varied. As such, the microfinance market must look more trustingly towards the traditional financial systems. The expansion of a network between the non-profit sector and the profit sector could help the search for other alternative solutions, which are able to exploit all the process and products financial innovations that are available in more developed financial markets.[5] On the other hand, so far the policies to expand sustainability here described are actually implemented by a very small number of formal MFIs. The creation of a structured network and a greater collaboration between MFIs and financial intermediaries would allow semi-formal institutions to improve their own operations and to enhance their operating and management standards. These solutions would help to avoid the consolidation of the microfinance market, in the near future, in a few agents, who are better organized and structured than many MFIs operating at present.

4.7 Conclusion

The search for a balance between sustainability objectives of microfinance institutions and the pursuit of social aims represents a trade-off in microfinance. This contrast is inspired by two different theoretical approaches, namely the Financial Service Approach and the Poverty Lending Approach, on the basis of which microfinance is seen either as a method of diversifying the offer of financial services to financially excluded individuals, or as an instrument to support the development of the poorest sectors of the population.

However, the microfinance institutions that are actually sustainable are, in practice, very few. Most MFIs benefit from subsidies in different forms. Consequently, the discussion between supporters of sustainability and defenders of outreach seems best represented by a scheme in which some MFIs focus on the social mission, while others put the economic mission first. This means that the first type of institutions must be subsidized, whereas the second can go towards self-sufficiency, which, to be achieved, must include specific strategies.

The analysis of the determining factors of sustainability and outreach has shown that there are operating and management policies that can bring together these apparently conflicting objectives. Traditional

policies can be aided by more innovative solutions when microfinance operators form profitable collaborations with banks and other financial intermediaries. An integrated network for microfinance represents the most advanced and tangible way towards sustainable outreach.

Finally, as a result of the issues discussed in this chapter, it is important to stress that microfinance cannot be considered an effective tool in every operational context. The offer of financial services to financially excluded individuals yields substantial results where lack of credit represents the main limit to the development of microenterprises and of self-employment. Conversely, when the lack of capital is accompanied by a significant deficiency in production or distribution processes, the supply of microcredits risks being a palliative for MFIs' beneficiaries; even those institutions that put social aims before economic ones, in such conditions of low productive efficiency, should opt first for initiatives based on donations rather than on supply of funds to be repaid.

5
Risk Management in Microfinance

Mario La Torre

5.1 Introduction

The new modern microfinance trend calls for the redesign of micro-finance risk management. The literature has paid little attention to risk analysis in microfinance. Moreover, it has focused mainly on credit risk and fraud risks. But the particular nature of microfinance, the complexity of modern financial structures, the variety of beneficiaries and institutions involved require a more structured approach of risk management. This chapter aims to lay the basis for a risk management model that could fit modern microfinance. In order to achieve this, the first step is to set a taxonomy of risk for microfinance. The idea is to make an overview of the different risks and to catalogue them according to the typical risk categories defined by banking regulation, with particular reference to the new Capital Accord of Basel II, which aims to 'secure international convergence on revisions to supervisory regulations governing the capital adequacy of international active banks' (Basel Committee on Banking Supervision, 2004a).

The chapter outlines the basic financial management policies for each specific risk category, distinguishing between a project financing approach and a portfolio approach. The first category deals with risk management of single projects, mainly promoted by non-formal and semi-formal institutions (mostly NGOs); a portfolio approach refers principally to semi-formal and formal MFIs who develop large-scale activities. The chapter does not consider the implementation of risk measuring models.

5.2   A taxonomy of risks for microfinance

The word 'risk' comes from the vulgar Latin 'rescum', which can be said to mean 'risk' or 'danger'. In finance, this leads to the concept of 'compensation': the expression *risk–return trade-off* implies that to bear the risk one needs to be compensated. This approach, however, can lead to a false concept of risk, in associating it only with negative events that can determine financial losses. Risk is, in fact, the uncertainty related to future events or future outcomes. This uncertainty does not mean that the event, or the outcome, must be negative. The compensation for bearing the risk is a premium for beating on the sign of the future event (outcome), not compensation for the loss to be registered. The notion of *risk–return trade-off* implies that to invest in a higher risk activity, a higher return is required. A rational investor, then, would be interested in measuring *ex ante* the level of risk associated with each investment in order to estimate the *risk–return trade-off* and to decide whether to invest and at what price. Since rational investors incorporate expected changes in their decisions, the effective risks arise only from unexpected changes.

Risk management, then, deals with the definition, the measurement and the control of risks (expected and unexpected changes) in order to price the investment correctly and to reduce losses determined by changes in future events or outcomes.

The scarce attention dedicated to risk management in microfinance can be explained mainly by the fact that the main goal of microfinance lies in social and humanitarian objectives. This approach, together with the dependency from public subsidies, has created a tendency to underestimate the financial performance of microfinance programmes or institutions. In recent years, the need for private resources has stimulated a growing awareness among practitioners of the concept of sustainability. This has lead, both in literature and in practice, to the development of performance evaluating models but has not necessitated the definition of risk management models. Identifying the risks, measuring them and controlling the exposure to these risks allows us to better identify the key variables that affect performance, and to implement the financial and operational solutions in order to reduce the performance variability. Moreover, there is a great need for a risk management model for microfinance, since the market is experiencing a stronger interaction between informal and semi-formal MFIs (mainly non-profit organizations and NGOs) and traditional financial intermediaries accustomed to risk management.

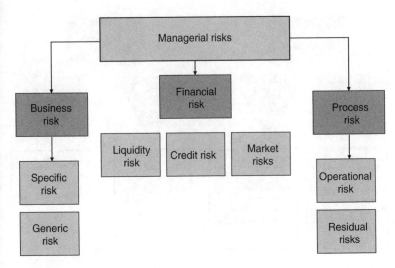

Figure 5.1 Risks in microfinance

Therefore, the first step for a risk management model is to identify the risk categories that refer to microfinance. It is possible to classify microfinance managerial risks into three key categories (Figure 5.1): *business risk* refers to the activity itself; *financial risks* derive from the portfolio of assets and from the liabilities associated with the project or stored in the institution's balance sheet; *process risk* includes all those risks determined by the process designed to implement the activity.

5.3 The business risk

Business risk results from the unique nature of microfinance. It can be split into two components: *specific risk* (product risk) and *generic risk* (Figure 5.2). Specific risk arises from the products and services offered. From an economic point of view, a microfinance programme can be defined as a prototype: each single programme is different from the others. Each programme has been developed to reach different categories of beneficiaries, located in different regions, with different culture and customs and, often, without any managerial experience or entrepreneurial background. This forces practitioners and institutions to invent new financial structures and to adapt the supply to the specific needs of the customers. This flexibility, which is a specific characteristic of microfinance compared to traditional finance, makes it particularly difficult to estimate *ex ante* the effectiveness of the products offered, the

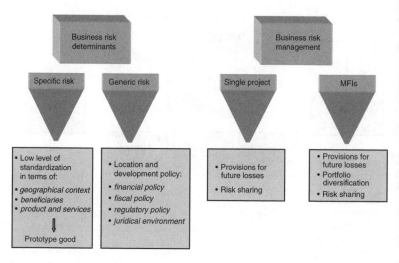

Figure 5.2 Business risk

efficiency of the financial structure implemented, as well as the costs and risks associated with the services. From a risk management perspective, business risk is mainly determined by the impossibility to reach a higher level of product standardization, a fact emphasized by the ethical goal of microfinance, which prioritizes the beneficiaries' needs, rather than institutional strategies.

Generic risk derives mostly from the location of the programme. It bears no relation to country risk (which is a component of credit risk) but refers to the development policy implemented in the area of activity. The risk comes from the possibility that the geographical context in which the programme is based is not supported, at an international or local level, by adequate financial, fiscal and regulatory policies, or that it can be affected by a change in these policies that would hinder the development of the programme. The risk determinant here is the possibility of a conflict between the financial, fiscal, juridical and regulatory environment and the programme itself, mainly deriving from a change in the development policy of governments and local bodies, as well as international institutions and donors, for a specific area.

The management of business risk is a complicated task for many reasons. First, it is worth pointing out that this kind of risk cannot be avoided. This is a consequence of the essence of microfinance, which operates in difficult contexts by helping people who live in poverty and who are victims of financial exclusion. MFIs don't have the option of choosing forms of investment that do not involve any substantial (relatively high

probability) business risk. Secondly, business risk, both in its specific or general meaning, is very difficult to evaluate, as it is generated by qualitative and unpredictable variables. This should lead MFIs and practitioners to take a very prudential approach when dealing with business risk and to ensure they always make provisions for future potential losses.

Business risk can also be managed through diversification or through sharing. Here, we must distinguish the case of a single project from that of an MFI. In a single project approach, it is very difficult (if not impossible) to implement a diversification strategy, either by geographic area, beneficiaries or other dimensions. Conversely, for an MFI, the likelihood of a diversified portfolio increases together with the volume of its activity. Risk sharing is the most feasible alternative when dealing with a single project and is good practice when dealing with a loan portfolio. Risk sharing allows business risk to be split between the lender and a third counter-party, normally an insurance company. This way of splitting the risk allows the lender to confine his exposure to the business risk inherent in the project, or in the pool of loans, to a minimum. Nevertheless, insurance companies do not offer products tailored for these specific needs and when they do, they do so at very high prices. Therefore, the availability of specific financial products and the opportunity cost related to them are the main stumbling blocks for business risk management in microfinance. Consequently, the role of governments and local authorities, as well as international donors, could be of great help, by allocating part of the money granted to donors to a business guarantee fund. This would result in a saving, since the risk events could never happen. At the same time, a guarantee fund would facilitate the attraction of private funds. In this way, investors would be able to choose forms of investment which do not involve any substantial business risk.

5.4   Financial risks

Within this category it is possible to classify all the risks deriving from the financial intermediation process. Financial intermediation consists of the transfer of funds from surplus units to deficit units. NGOs and MFIs channel funds obtained from donors, investors or depositors to beneficiaries. Thus, they run the same financial risks borne by traditional financial intermediaries. These risks are normally classified as *liquidity risk*, *credit risk* and *market risk*. For years, researchers and microfinance practitioners have focused their attention on credit risk, underestimating liquidity risk and simply not considering market risk. The nature of

microfinance services (mainly represented by microcredit), the funding policies carried out by NGOs and other MFIs (mainly based on public funds) and the non-formal or semi-formal nature of the institutions involved in microfinance business have been the main reasons for this attitude. Moreover, the management of credit risk has been influenced by a biased attitude towards microfinance beneficiaries and by the dichotomy of the two goals of sustainability and outreach more than being inspired by economic and financial variables. Over the last few years the growing number MFIs assuming the nature of semi-formal or formal institutions, together with the introduction of commercial banks in the microfinance market, has encouraged the building of risk management models for microfinance which have the same status as the ones used by regulated financial institutions. The aim of this section is to analyse the three categories of financial risks described above following the traditional approach used in literature for banks and financial intermediaries, and to outline the main differences, in terms of determinants, that characterize microfinance compared with traditional finance.

5.4.1   Liquidity risk

Liquidity risk can be defined as the risk arising from changes in cash flow. Thus, the risk is composed of an expected component and an unexpected one. The risk of liquidity management has a quantitative impact and a qualitative one: the quantity element focuses on whether or not there is liquidity to meet obligations; the qualitative factor has to deal with the price at which liquidity can be obtained, or with the opportunity cost at which liquidity can be stored in the balance sheet. *Therefore, liquidity risk can be defined as the risk of not having cash to meet obligations, as well as the price or the opportunity cost or loss to bear in order to obtain cash.* For financial institutions, the need for a cushion of liquidity comes from the necessity of meeting customers' liquidity requirements, such as deposit withdrawals or new loan demands, and operational expenses. It is the unexpected change in these two variables that produces liquidity risk.

Banks and financial intermediaries have to estimate liquidity needs, and changes in these needs (expected and unexpected). If a bank could predict the exact timing and number of uses of funds it would be easier to synchronize them with sources of funds. In the real world expected and actual changes are rarely equal. The existence of unexpected changes determines the risk that a bank will not be able to synchronize sources and uses of funds. The purpose of liquidity management is to

avoid liquidity crises. Hence, liquidity needs should be met without costly disruptions.

In order to budget future cash flow, it is important to identify the main variables that can determine expected and unexpected inflows and outflows. Cash flow can be generated by non-discretionary conversion of assets and liabilities into cash (when there is no explicit decision by the institution) and by discretionary conversion of funds. A bank, for example, records inflows from non-discretionary asset conversion, when loans and securities mature and the bank receives principal and interest payments (self-liquidating assets), and from discretionary decisions, such as conversion of liquid assets into cash (reserves, bonds, shares, loans) or the issuing of new liabilities. Cash outflows derive mainly from non-discretionary deposit withdrawals or loans withdrawals and from discretionary actions, such as the granting of new loans, debt repayments and operational expenses. Thus, the liquidity risk can be expressed by equation 5.1:

$$CCFt = (ENC + EDC) + (UNC + UDC) \tag{5.1}$$

where:

$CCFt$ = cash flow change in period t
ENC = expected non-discretionary change
EDC = expected discretionary change
UNC = unexpected non-discretionary change
UDC = unexpected discretionary change

To address the management of liquidity risk in microfinance, we must distinguish the case of a single project from the case of an institution. The case of a single project refers mostly to an informal provider or to a semi-formal institution, mainly an NGO, carrying out a small number of programmes with separate accounting systems or, in a few cases, to a formal MFI adopting a project financing approach. In both situations, cash inflows are determined by the funds attracted to set up and develop the project and by loan repayments. Cash outflows are generated by operational expenses and loans granted (Figure 5.3).

There are two main differences compared with a bank cash flow system. The variables that generate the cash flow are less than those of a bank, thus the nondiscretionary and unexpected components in cash flow changes play a less important role. Non-discretionary and

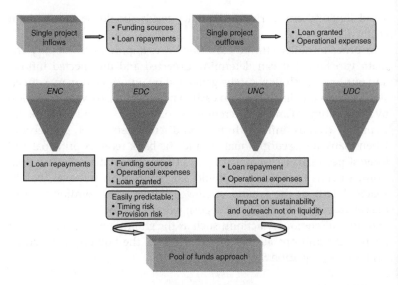

Figure 5.3   Liquidity risk: a single project approach

unexpected changes can derive only from loans repayments and operational expenses. Nevertheless, these changes do not seriously affect liquidity. The rate of default on loans is usually lower than the rate experienced by commercial banks. Moreover, repayments on loans are not assigned to cover operational expenses, which are generally financed by a specific percentage of the funds that set up the programme. Thus, changes in loan repayments affect only the loan portfolio: less liquidity is equal to a lower number of new loans. In the same way, an unexpected growth of operational expenses would be covered by the donation obtained. This will not result in a shortage of cash but it will reduce the amount of money available for new loans. Unexpected changes in loan repayments and in operational expenses, therefore, will have a greater impact on the sustainability and outreach of the project than on its liquidity.

Expected and discretionary changes derive from funding sources, loans and operational expenses. On the funding side, a single project is usually supported by subsidies or soft loans, whose amount is agreed and usually available at the start of the project. Therefore, expected changes in funding are usually easily predictable. With reference to the outflow, the amount of loans and financial services to be supplied, as well as the amount of operational expenses, is established during the planning phase of the project. Moreover, the granting of new loans,

during the life of the project, is strictly correlated to the size of the revolving fund which depends on the performance of the project: if no money is reimbursed by the first loan portfolio then no new loan will be granted and no liquidity needs will arise. In the same way, if expected changes in operational expenses arise, they will be funded by donations. Therefore, liquidity risk can arise only when donations are not available at the start of the programme or if the provisions for future expected exchanges on operational expenses are insufficient.

Cash flow budgeting for a project is considerably less complicated than it is for a bank and can be focused mainly on the first part (and in particular the *EDC* component) of equation 5.1.

In the case of an MFI, liquidity management becomes more complex and more similar to a bank's liquidity management, as we move from a semiformal to a formal institution (Figure 5.4). Different sources of funds, on the liability side, loan portfolios and other financial investments, on the asset side, lead to a more complex structure of the balance sheet and determine a more complex cash flow budget. Moreover, operational expenses give a higher contribution to outflows. Here, non-discretionary and unexpected changes play a significant role in liquidity risk.

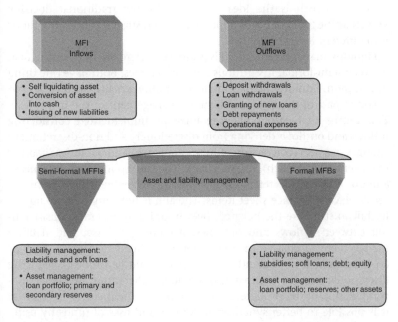

Figure 5.4 Liquidity risk for MFIs

Managing liquidity risk is, then, a different task when dealing with the budget of a single project or a balance sheet of an institution. The key variable to focus on when managing liquidity risk for a microfinance project is the relationship between the funds attracted, on one side, and the loan portfolio and the operational expenses on the other. In this case the aim is to strike a balance, in terms of amount and timing, between the inflow generated by the donors' funds, and the outflow related to operational expenses and the financial products offered to beneficiaries. Since, when the programme starts, there is no uncertainty regarding the amount of subsidies obtained and the amount of money to be granted, liquidity management must focus mainly on the timing in which the funds may be effectively available, and on the evaluation of the expected changes in operational expenses. Thus, it is important to adopt a prudential approach and not to underestimate the time needed to get the money from donors and of the provision for operational expenses. This solution represents an alternative to liquidity reserves provision funded within the project or with funds coming from other projects (cross-subsidization). In this case, liquidity management becomes, principally, the practice of storing primary reserves (cash) or secondary reserves (mainly short-term treasury bills) to avoid cash shortages, which is the idea supported by the traditional doctrine known as the 'pool of funds approach', which suggests allocating funds into different levels of reserves.

Liquidity management for MFIs is different. Here, we must distinguish between semi-formal institutions and formal ones. Both have one thing in common: liquidity management is not only a matter or reserves but becomes part of the asset and liability management of the institution. This means that cash budgeting must be implemented considering inflows and outflows deriving from discretionary and non-discretionary changes in assets (conversion of funds approach) and liabilities (liability management approach), like in a bank. The correspondence, in terms of amount and timing, refers to inflow and outflow generated from the most relevant balance sheet items. The aim is not only to store liquidity but to structure the balance sheet in order to minimize mismatching between inflows and outflows. According to asset and liability management, a change in nondiscretionary items (a deposit drain or an increase in loan demand, for example) could be offset by reducing discretionary assets, increasing discretionary liabilities, or choosing a combination of the two alternatives. Moreover, the theory suggests that it is possible to better synchronize sources and uses of funds by using flows of non-discretionary payments deriving from non-discretionary

assets, such as interest and payment stream from loans and long-term securities.

Naturally, formal institutions have a more complex balance sheet structure compared with semi-formal ones. They can take deposits and, usually, they do not have investment restrictions. Therefore, for formal MFIs cash flow determinants are the same as for banks. Cash flow budgeting becomes more complex but, at the same time, the institution has more alternatives to avoid cash flow mismatching. Like banks, formal MFIs generate inflows both from self-liquidating assets and from discretionary conversion of funds, as well as from the opening of new deposit accounts. This approach leads to a cost–opportunity analysis of the different solutions available to avoid cash shortages. Thus, the main differences between semi-formal and formal institutions are twofold. First, semi-formal institutions cannot offer deposit services and are subject to investment restrictions. Therefore, liability management is focused on funding mix strategies oriented mainly to subsidies, and soft loans, whereas asset management is focused on loan portfolios and primary and secondary reserves. Secondly, semi-formal institutions are not always required by a supervisory authority to respect liquidity requirements and, if so, these requirements consist in liquidity ratios that indicate the level of cash reserves. Conversely, liquidity requirements are more stringent for formal MFIs. When under banking regulation, formal MFIs in most developed countries are subject to rules that ensure a correspondence between the maturity of the assets and the maturity of liabilities stored in the balance sheet, not only to liquidity ratios.

Yet, in most developing countries, microfinance regulators require semi-formal and formal MFIs to respect only the traditional reserve ratios calculated as a specific percentage of total deposits. This approach does not differ very much from the basic approach outlined for the management of a single project, with the sole difference that, in this case, reserve requirements are compulsory. The balance sheet structure of many semi-formal and formal MFIs would require a banking supervision approach. In these cases, the responsibility for liquidity management rests principally on a voluntary internal regulation rather then external supervision imposed by authorities. MFIs, semi-formal and formal, should adopt an asset and liability approach to managing liquidity risk. In this case, equation 5.1 would lead not simply to a standard liquidity ratio but to an equation ensuring the match between assets and liabilities (equations 5.2 and 5.3):

$$LTA = LTL + \% \, MTL + \% \, STL \tag{5.2}$$
$$MTA = D + (1 - \% \, MLT) + (1 - \% \, SLT) \tag{5.3}$$

where:

> LTA = long-term assets
> LTL = long-term liabilities
> MTL = medium-term liabilities
> STL = short-term liabilities
> MTA = medium-term assets
> $D = LTA - (LTL + \% \, MTL + \% \, STL)$

5.4.2   Credit risk

Credit risk is usually defined as the risk that the borrower will not pay back interest and/or principal. In fact, credit risk has a much broader meaning. *It is the risk of an unexpected change in the creditworthiness of the borrower that may lead to a lower value of the loan or to a loss.* Credit risk is, then, not only the risk of a loss referred to a specific exposure but refers also to the downgrading of the borrower. As such, credit risk cannot be represented by a binomial distribution of two possible events (insolvency or solvency of the borrower), but is better represented by a discreet distribution in which the insolvency is the extreme outcome of a different number of downgrading stages. Thus, the determinant of credit risk is the unexpected change in the creditworthiness of the borrower. The effect of credit risk may be a lower return caused by a downgrading of the borrower, not compensated by higher spreads than the market would require (*opportunity cost effect*), or a loss determined both by the insolvency of the borrower (*insolvency loss effect*) or by the transfer of the loan at discount (*sale loss effect*). Among these effects, academia and managers have focused mainly on the insolvency loss effect, which is the most common and most evident consequence of credit risk. Thus, since borrowers never pay back more than they get, credit risk is defined as an asymmetric risk, meaning that it reflects an asymmetric distribution of expected returns. In microfinance, the insolvency loss effect is the most relevant element of credit risk for two principal reasons: microcredits do not have secondary markets that could give rise to sale loss effect, and, usually, the pricing of microcredit it is not strictly correlated to market rates, making opportunity cost effect irrelevant.

The last point leads us to one of the main features of microfinance credit policy, which plays a crucial role in credit risk: the *non-rationing approach*. Banks and financial intermediaries do not lend at any price; beyond a certain point, in fact, higher interest rates create *adverse*

selection: when interest rates are relatively high, best-quality borrowers are not willing to borrow money and banks are subjected to the risk of lending to worst-quality customers. Conversely, MFIs have the specific task of lending money to borrowers whose perceived creditworthiness is relatively weak. Therefore, they actually behave in the opposite way to banks. This may lead to two different approaches: opting for a lower expected return or, alternatively, applying very high interest rates. This recalls the issue of the ethical approach for microfinance discussed in Chapter 1. Microfinance literature and practitioners seem to justify a flexible interest rate policy, not subject to interest rate caps, arguing that microfinance is not charity and that microfinance lending must foster an attitude of financial responsibility among borrowers, together with a goal of sustainability of the microfinance programme. Nevertheless, loan pricing policy in microfinance has been inspired mainly by an *ex ante* perceived creditworthiness of the borrower more than by a valuation of the effective credit risk related to the loan. This paragraph aims to analyse the main components of credit risk, as explained by the literature and by prudential regulation implemented by banks and financial intermediaries. This could help managers and practitioners in developing credit risk models for microfinance which could facilitate the evaluation of customer creditworthiness, and would finally foster a more accurate pricing of microcredits. We believe that this would not necessarily lead to high interest rates and commission, and would partially help in minimizing the dichotomy between outreach and sustainability.

Credit risk is determined by two components (Figure 5.5): the *expected loss* (*EL*) and the *unexpected loss* (*UL*). The *EL* is represented by the mean value of loss distribution for a certain category of loans; the *UL* is the variability around that mean. Since rational managers incorporate expected changes in their decision making and, more specifically, in loan pricing, risk arises mainly from unexpected losses, that is to say, that the variability is the financial management measure of the risk. While banks and financial intermediaries adopt different statistical models to calculate the *EL* and the *UL*, and banking supervision rules use these statistical variables to define bank capital requirements against credit risk, MFIs do not normally approach credit risk management from this perspective. Nevertheless, *EL* and *UL* are significant variables to estimate the potential credit loss. Estimating future values of *EL* and *UL* is useful for forecasting the possible value of future losses.

The estimate of *EL* related to credit exposure requires the evaluation of three variables (equation 5.4): the *adjusted exposure* (*AE*), the *probability of*

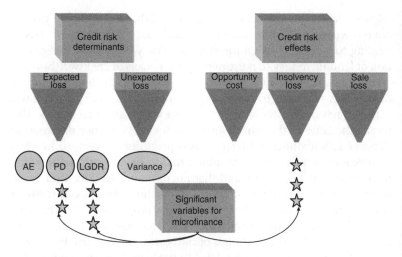

Figure 5.5   Credit risk determinants and effects
Note: * indicates degree of relevance.

default (PD) and the *loss given default rate* (LGDR):

$$EL = AE \times PD \times LGDR \qquad (5.4)$$

where the *AE* is the effective exposure at default, the *PD* is the mean value of loss distribution for a specific loan category, and *LGDR* is the expected loss rate calculated in percentage of the recovery rate (1 − recovery rate). In microfinance lending, these three variables take on different meanings with respect to traditional lending.

AE is much more predictable for MFIs than for banks. This is because *AE* depends essentially on the specific loan product and, in particular, on the flexibility that the borrower has in drawing money from the credit facility granted. The bigger this flexibility is, the higher the risk *exposure* of the lender, and the more difficult it is to predict the *AE*. In this case, in fact, the lender must estimate the undrawn portion of the loan that will be drawn at the moment of default (equation 5.5):

$$AE = DP + UP \times UGD \qquad (5.5)$$

where:

DP = drawn portion
UP = undrawn portion
UGD = usage given default

Microfinance, generally, designs loan products with one single withdrawal at the concession of the loan and does not allow borrowers for ongoing discharges. Therefore, microfinance lending runs no *exposure risk*, and there is no *UP* and *UGD* to consider in the computation of *AE*.

PD expresses the credit rating of the borrower; the probability of default is a proxy for the creditworthiness of the borrower which depends primarily on his character, his economic and financial profile, and his business profile. *PD* is, then, calculated using historical statistics on default rate for homogeneous categories of borrowers. In that case, the mean default rate is taken as a proxy of the PD of future borrowers. In microfinance, the estimate of PD is complicated by the lack of reliable statistics and by the difficulty of structuring homogeneous sets of data diversified by borrower categories and by geographical criteria. Theoretically speaking, if compared to traditional lending, microcredit should be associated with higher *PD*. This is mainly because of the particular nature of microfinance beneficiaries and the country risk component. The country risk accounts for all the factors that may determine a default event not directly dependent on the borrower himself but mainly on the economical, social and political situation of the country in which the borrower's activity is based. This risk component plays a significant role in microfinance credit risk, especially for those loans situated in developing countries. Nevertheless, many programmes and many MFIs around the world have shown very low *ex post* default rates. This evidence is in stark contrast with the interest rates and the commissions applied to borrowers. The implementation of statistical methodology to estimate *PD* for microfinance borrowers would probably facilitate a more accurate pricing of microcredits.

LGDR indicates the loss rate that the lender effectively bears after the default event has occurred. This is the most critical component of *EL*, when talking about microcredit. *LGDR* depends mostly on the ability of the lender to recover as much as possible from the borrower after his default. This ability depends on different factors: the guarantees that assist the loan, the nature of the business financed, the legal and administrative environment that influences the recovery process. Furthermore, the recovery rate relies on two variables: the recovery rate on the loan itself (mostly dependent on collateral), and the opportunity cost, expressed by the administrative costs associated to the recovery procedure and the time needed to complete the whole process. Microfinance lending is characterized by the lack of traditional guarantees and, moreover, generally takes place in geographical contexts that do not ensure a legal environment that allows for transparent and rapid

recovery procedures. For these reasons, microfinance lending is associated with a higher rate of *LGDR* compared with traditional lending.

The *UL* is the variance on the mean of the *EL*. Therefore, it is dependent on the variance of *AE*, *PD* and *LGDR*. *The estimate of UL* is rather complicated and requires sophisticated statistical models. The underlying idea behind these models is to forecast a worst case scenario for the variance of each of the three variables and fix a correspondent confidence interval. In this way, it is possible to estimate the maximum loss, for a certain probability, that may occur in the worst scenario. What is relevant, for microfinance, is that the most significant component of *UL* is again the *LGDR*, which is presumed to show the highest variance around the mean. Conversely, *AE* does not imply variance, according to the traditional microfinance lending products, while *PD* is supposed to show different values of its variance in relation to different programmes or loan portfolios.

Thus, microfinance credit risk management implies the management of *EL* and *UL*, as in traditional lending. This can be achieved under a single loan approach or considering a loan portfolio (Figure 5.6).

With regard to a single loan, the management of credit risk requires essentially two steps. First, a review analysis of the customer creditworthiness and the market in which it operates, before credit is granted; secondly, a continuous monitoring and servicing process, once the loan has been granted.[1] Creditworthiness analysis is the key variable for *EL*; it indicates the level of *PD* associated with the borrower, it gives indications on the amount to grant, in order to fix a measure of *AE* coherent with the level of *PD*, and on the guarantees needed to minimize *LGDR*. With regard to banking lending, in microfinance creditworthiness analysis is much more dependent on qualitative variables, both when considering the borrower's creditworthiness or the collateral that support the loan. This makes it more difficult to estimate *PD* and *LGDR* but, at the same time, suggests a method for future consideration: the developing of qualitative credit score models. The monitoring process, on the contrary, assumes great importance with reference to *LGDR* and *UL*. When conveniently structured, it helps to minimize the size of unexpected losses and to maximize the recovery rate.

When considering a loan portfolio, *EL* and *UL* can be managed also through portfolio policy. On the one side, *EL* cannot be eliminated but only stabilized through increasing the loan portfolio. This policy can be easily pursued by a formal MFI, while it is a hard task for NGOs or institutions working under a single project financing approach. On the other hand, *UL* can be significantly minimized through a diversification policy that allows the reduction of the mean variance of all the *EL*

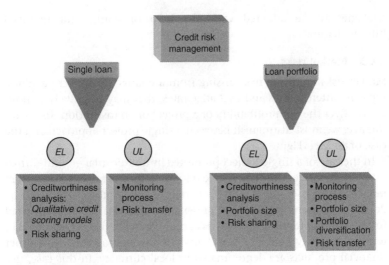

Figure 5.6 Credit risk management

components. This aspect is critical also for MFIs.; for their nature and dimension, while they do not bear as great an exposure risk as banks do, they generally tend to concentrate the credit risk on their portfolio, either by geographic area, business segment or beneficiaries category. In other words, they tend to concentrate their activity in those segments in which they have developed greater experience and skill. This element of concentration leads to an undiversified portfolio. In such circumstances, the likelihood that credit losses may have significant consequences on the institutions stability is very high.

Large loan portfolios and portfolio diversification are, then, complex tasks for MFIs and make credit risk management more difficult than it is for banks. This is one of the reasons that has encouraged many MFIs to take the form of a traditional bank. Of course, this is a reasonable alternative, but only for a few institutions. For the majority of MFIs, credit risk management can be pursued mainly through creditworthiness analysis or financial innovation. Future energy, in this field, must be focused on the developing of qualitative credit score models and the structuring of risk-transferring financial products. In consequence, it is possible to imagine a more widespread use of guarantee funds offered by governmental bodies or municipalities, wider access to insurance products offered by insurance companies, especially tailored for country risk, or recourse to credit derivatives and asset-backed securitization

strategies to be adopted with the help of banks and financial intermediaries.

5.4.3 Market risks

Market risks are those risks arising from a change in market variables, typically interest rates and exchange rates, that may negatively or positively affect the net profitability of a project or an institution. In microfinance, we must distinguish between a single project approach and the case of an MFI (Figure 5.7).

In the case of a single project promoted by an informal or semi-formal institution, interest rate risk is linked to interest rates to be received from microcredits (asset sensitivity). Generally, a single project is funded by donors and, therefore, does not present the financial expenses incurred from borrowed funds. Currency risk arises when the project is funded in foreign currency (liability sensitivity), while microcredits and other financial products are denominated in local currency. In this case, risk management should follow a micro-hedging approach, which aims to manage the single financial exposure (related to the loan portfolio and to the donations) for interest rate risk and for currency risk respectively. The simplicity of microfinance programmes, and the limited/small amount of money usually invested, leads to a choice of two alternatives in a cost–opportunity evaluation: either, to bear the risk, simply making

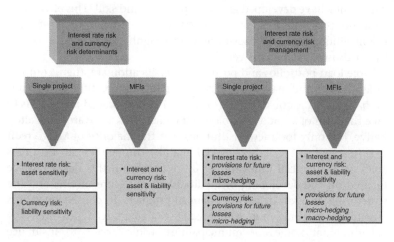

Figure 5.7 Market risks

provisions for future losses, or to go for very simple and non-costly micro-hedging.

It is worth pointing out, anyway, that in the case of single projects, interest risk impacts only on the loan portfolio. Interest rates on loans are not used to cover either financial expenses (there are no borrowed funds) or operational expenses (which are covered by a specific percentage of donations) but are used for funding future loans: therefore, a lower amount of interest received, because of a change in interest rates, means a lower amount of future credits granted. Moreover, in practice, when a project is funded by donors, changes in market interest rates usually do not imply changes in interest rates applied to borrowers. Thus, there is no unexpected change in the flow of interest received because of a change in market rates and, therefore, no interest rate risk. With reference to currency risk, it is worth remembering that local currency is usually weaker than the donor's; therefore, an exchange rate appreciation would impact positively both on operational expenses expressed in local currency and on the amount of money originally assigned to the loan portfolio.

MFIs, in particular formal ones, have a more complex structure. They usually have large loan portfolios and other investments on the assets side of their balance sheet; borrowed funds and equity on the liability side. In this case, market risks can be better managed following both a micro-hedging and a macro-hedging approach, which looks at the exposure of the whole balance sheet. These institutions do not differ very much from a bank and, therefore, should adopt the same models developed by banks to measure and control market risk.

5.5 Process risks

Process risk will be analysed in more detail in Chapter 6. Here, a theoretical framework is offered which is useful for understanding the ways in which it can affect the performance of a microfinance programme or of a MFI. The literature offers different taxonomies of process risks, each of which are acceptable and comprehensive. We decided to adopt the classification closest to banking regulation provisions, and in particular the one proposed by the Basel 2 Accord. This choice has the advantage of opting for a standardization of management risk approach between MFIs and other financial intermediaries.

Process risks can be distinguished into two main categories: *operational risks* and other *residual risks* (Figure 5.8). The Basel Committee on Banking Supervision defines operational risks as 'the risk of loss resulting

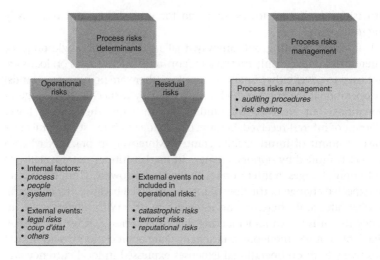

Figure 5.8 Process risks

from inadequate or failed internal processes, people and systems or for external events' (Basel Committee on Banking Supervision, 2001b). This definition, tailored for banks, can be adopted for MFIs and microfinance projects, as well. This specific perspective distinguishes two main components of operational risks: the risk arising from internal factors and the risk arising from external determinants. Internal events can be associated with the production process (under an efficiency and efficacy perspective), to people and their behaviour (workers, contractors, customers), to systems and their running (technological infrastructures). External determinants refers to all the events (mainly legal risks) that cannot be directly associated with the process or the institution. The category of other residual risks explains all the risks that do not fit in the Basel definitions of operational risks. They refer mostly to all the external events not included in operational risks, such as catastrophic risk, terrorist risks and reputational risk.

The common feature of operational and residual risk is that they are negative unintentional risks. MFIs, or an institution promoting a single microfinance project, cannot avoid these risks: to avoid them the only option is not to carry out the activity. Moreover, the effect of process risks can be only a loss since process risks are not speculative risks: therefore, a higher level of process risks does not mean, *ex ante*, a higher

level of return. Thus, the management of process risk becomes even more significant. In microfinance this evidence is still more critical for at least three reasons. First, MFIs and microfinance projects are characterized by a great flexibility in their organizational and operational structure. This element is generally associated with weak controls on production process, which is an area of potential operational risks. Secondly, the great involvement of non-profit organization corresponds, generally, to weak controls on human behaviour, leaving great space for fraud risk, which is another significant determinant of operational and reputational risks. Finally, MFIs and microfinance projects are often based in geographic areas that bear a high level of catastrophic and terrorist risks and, therefore, are naturally exposed to residual risks.

There are two main ways of managing process risks: the implementation of internal auditing procedures and the transfer of the risk to an external entity. The first option faces the difficulty of structuring procedures for control that do not meet with the flexibility needed by microfinance practitioners. The second solution can be pursued only if, and when, financial markets offer products specifically tailored for microfinance process risks and when a cost–opportunity analysis suggests this course of action.

5.6 Conclusion

The reasons above explain why risk management is becoming a key issue in modern microfinance. The need to reach new categories of beneficiaries has stimulated MFIs to work for a more structured organization and for a more strict interaction with traditional financial intermediaries. On the one hand, a diversified supply of financial services has led to more sophisticated microfinance programmes; on the other hand, the presence of profit-oriented intermediaries has stressed the relevance of self-sustainable projects. Thus, risk management becomes a key variable for a successful microfinance, both with reference to single projects or to the efficiency and stability of MFIs and the market itself. The measure and the management of business risk, as financial and process risks, is the way to minimize negative effects on performance; it also allows for a more correct pricing of the services offered. As such, it is also possible to state that MFIs, with respect to traditional banks, have a moral obligation to implement modern risk management systems. Being aware of their overall risk exposure, they can apply interest rates and commissions referring them to a more accurate risk estimate and not only to a perceived *ex ante* and subjective evaluation of customer creditworthiness.

An accurate pricing policy, together with risk management measures, could allow, in some cases, for less restrictive financial conditions applied to beneficiaries, without compromising self-financial sustainability. Risk management is a way to verify under which circumstances sustainability does not come into conflict with outreach. In other words, it is a way to verify under which circumstances microfinance can be ethical and sustainable at the same time.

6
Monitoring the Microfinance Processes

Monica Ortolani

6.1 Introduction

The distinguishing elements of microfinance compared with traditional finance, as pointed out in the previous chapters, are the target clients and the typology of the offered products. The satisfaction of the various needs of the clients, located in different geographic locations, has led to the development of many typologies of microfinance institutions characterized by more or less structured products – sometimes including non-financial products – which also follow socio-ethical exigencies. Therefore, the operational processes that are finalized to the achievement of the strategic objectives – both economic and social – of the different institutions have specific levels of standardization and complexity, and, consequently, the arrangement of the performed activities changes. The 'micro' features of the offered products and the simplicity of the methodologies used for their structuring and distribution is, indeed, the result of a number of activities that are carefully planned, organized and controlled. The operational processes' effectiveness and efficiency, despite the complexity of the supplying institution, widely depends on the existence and on the implementation of continuous monitoring and control systems for the activities as well as for the human resources and tangible assets that are used. Such systems must be correctly planned, implemented and shared at all organization levels, in order to guarantee that all activities are carried out correctly.

The aim of this chapter is to identify the typologies of control that allow a correct monitoring of activities and of human resources used during the production activities of microfinance, and also the monitoring of the related information system. In order to achieve this, at first the typical processes of microfinance are identified, focusing the attention

on microcredit, which is the most widespread process/product among microfinance institutions. Afterwards, the risks concerning effectiveness and efficiency are identified, focusing mainly on operational risks, since financial risks have been already analysed in Chapter 5. Finally, the key variables for a correct control and reporting system are chosen. This is to achieve, at various levels, the correct monitoring of the activities and the human resources to limit risks, while achieving the institutional objectives efficiently and effectively, focusing on the structural elements as well as on process elements. In such perspective, these issues will be explained without making distinctions between formal and semi-formal institutions, but keeping a process point of view. Such distinctions do not influence the need to adopt a control system and an information management system. Again, referring to the efficiency and the effectiveness of the processes and to the risks related to human resources, the incentive system is analysed; this is used very often as a functional instrument for the achievement of the performance objectives, but sometimes it can imply a relevant risk. In consideration of the above, we will try to answer the following questions: why is the incentive system so important in microfinance activities? Can the incentive system lead to *adverse selection* behaviours and increase the risk of fraud?

6.2 Reasons for a process approach

Although microfinance institutions have their typical objectives, clients and products, they operate according to the same effectiveness and efficiency criteria as traditional financial institutions. In order to achieve their objectives and to control the risks deriving from their operations, MFIs need to adopt an internal control system that allows the monitoring of the activities that are carried out and the related operating units.

Internal control system planning depends on the typologies of the activities that are implemented and, therefore, on the number of products and services they offer and on the human resources that are used; for each product/service there is generally a process that involves operating units to which are assigned tasks and responsibilities. Therefore, in order to define the best control system, it is necessary to identify the structural and process components and the existing relationship between them, especially in terms of information and reporting management system.

The control system is actually an instrument of active monitoring of operations and management and, consequently, it is not only configured as a control instrument, but also as a governance instrument. The internal control system also systematizes the complexity of the institution by controlling

risks, by monitoring the trends of the most important variables, and by creating an infrastructure that achieves an integrated management of all processes and of human resources involved in a common scheme.

The definition of the institution's structure consists in the identification of the single operating units involved in the institution's processes and in the assignment of tasks and responsibilities that derive from the organization of operations. *The definition of the institution's processes* concerns the organization of the necessary *flow of activities* and the identification of the related phases.

The link between *organizational structure* and *processes* is determined when the tasks and the responsibilities related to the single activities are assigned to the operating units. By doing so, it is easier to identify the risks that derive from the above-mentioned components, and, therefore, to plan the internal control system structure in order to be functional to the specific typology of institution, to its objectives and to the control of the specific risks. In light of the above, control activities apply to each flow of activity and to each operating unit involved, following the principle of tight relationship between structure and process components.

An effective and efficient internal control system is obviously supported by an information and reporting system that allows the circulation of the information deriving from the monitoring of activities and of operating units. Information and monitoring reports must circulate from the top to the bottom of the organizational structure and vice versa; in fact, by doing so, the control system enhances its governance function, finalized to optimize the management decision process in order to solve the problems promptly, before the achievement of the objectives is jeopardized. The system needs to be simple, transparent and appropriately scheduled in order to improve the actual operations of the institution at every organizational level.

6.3   Microfinance processes

MFIs' operations are characterized by the possibility of coexistence of financial activities as well as socio-ethical ones; for each one of these activities certain processes are structured up, in order to allow the production of the service and its distribution to the beneficiaries. This section only analyses the financial activities.

The processes of microfinance institutions are not different from those used by traditional banking intermediaries and are grouped according to the typical management areas in *Governance processes, Production activity processes, Support processes and Control processes* (Figure 6.1). The set of

```
Governance processes
Strategic planning
Operational planning
Commercial policies
Risk management policies
Definition of organizational structure
Definition of the internal control system
```

```
Production activity processes
Credit management
Saving management
Collections and payments management
Trading on financial market management
```

```
Support processes
Infrastructure management
Information technology management
Human resources management
Budgeting and management control
Top management reporting
Disclosure requirements management
```

```
Control processes
I level controls
II level controls
III level controls
```

Figure 6.1　MFIs' processes
Source:　adapted from Pesic (2005)

these four macro-categories of processes represents the map of the activities that are carried out inside the MFI; such macro-categories are always present, yet the number of processes may vary depending on the complexity of the specific institution, and is more structured for formal MFIs compared to semiformal and informal ones. We mainly refer to operations-related processes that depend on the products/services offered.

The identification of the above-mentioned processes also reveals the responsibilities of the operating units inside the organizational structure and, therefore, allows the identification of the control points, the tasks and the roles of the single units within the internal control system itself.

The *Governance processes* area includes all those activities, organized in processes, that are finalized to define the guidelines of the institution; therefore, these activities represent the decisional process of the top management. In particular, such processes define:

- the *strategic planning*, with the institution's medium- to long-term objectives, the risk–return profile for each production activity, the development plans, the target markets;

- the *operational planning*, with the specific objectives for each business unit, the risk–return objectives, the yearly budget, the investments and the expenses;
- the *commercial policies*, that is, the procedures through which the agreed objectives are achieved;
- the *risk management policies* which, depending on what has been agreed during the strategic planning, outline the procedures and the instruments used for the risk management, following the return objectives (see Chapter 5);
- the *definition of the organizational structure*, to adjust the structure of the institution to the needs that derive from the chosen objectives (i.e., the use of travelling loan officers in rural areas or suburbs);
- the *definition of the internal control system*, depending on the organizational structure and on the operational activities that are carried out.

The *Production activity processes* depend, as previously mentioned, on the quantity and typology of the services/products offered; to each product corresponds a process; the products that characterize MFIs' operations are *credit management, saving management, collections and payments management*. With regards to the process concerning the *trading on financial markets management*, we refer, in particular, to banks that operate in the microfinance sector. The *credit management* process surely represents the traditional and original process of microfinance, since microcredit is the main product offered by these institutions (see section 6.4). The *saving management* process identifies the typology of saving products that meet the needs of the target clients; the demand for these products is constantly increasing and has transformed many semi-formal institutions into formal ones. The *collections and payments management* process is aimed at meeting the needs regarding the transfer of clients' funds; in such context, the remittance issue is very important for those MFIs that operate with immigrant clients.

The *Support processes* include all the activities that allow the institution to carry out its work; they consist in cross-activities with the other processes. The *human resources management* activities are particularly important because they are a strategic element of microfinance; an important matter in such context is the incentives issue, which is handled in this process. The *budgeting and management control* process concerns the planning of activities and the monitoring of the management performance, using final period data and budget forecasting through which the monitoring on the level of achievement of the objectives is

performed. The *top management reporting* applies to the creation and management of information reports regarding the operations and management of single areas. Such system should include at least three levels. The first, regarding operations, should highlight the activities that are carried out and their compliance with the operational planning of reference; such activities are carried out by each single operational unit (i.e., loan officers). The second level derives from the mergence of many operative reports and it concerns the related management area (such reports are written by the managers of each single area). The third level synthesizes the flow of information of the other levels and provides the achievement of the strategic objectives; it is forwarded to the bank's management and, depending on the information it contains, it allows taking the appropriate decisions in order to improve the activities and to perform the necessary corrections to achieve the objectives. For formal institutions there are also disclosure requirements which are addressed to the supervisors.

The *Control processes* concern the first, second and third level controls. The typology of the controls will be deepened further on. For this process we simply have to point out that also control activities are organized in processes and the responsibilities have to be clearly defined and assigned to specific bodies. Such processes provide information and reports that support operational decision-making and the management of the institution. The monitoring activity concerns both the activities and the involved operating units.

Each process should be documented by a procedure, by a manual or by operating instructions that details the specific responsibilities.

6.4   The process of microcredit

Microcredit constitutes, without doubt, the most distributed product of all MFIs, whether they are formal, semi-formal or informal. The typology of institution involved, as well as the participation in development cooperation programmes, influences the complexity and the organization of the single activities, the product distribution and planning, but the process as such remains the same. The distinctive element of microcredit, regardless of the typology of supplying institution, is in the sought objective, that is, to satisfy the particular financial needs of the client through the planning and distribution of a product that has the characteristics suited to the satisfaction of this specific need (see Chapter 2), in an objective of effectiveness and efficiency, satisfying at the same time socio-ethical objectives not present in traditional lending, first and foremost

the credit access to financially excluded individuals. Despite the existence of various typologies of MFIs, more or less formalized and structured, in its essence the microcredit process corresponds to traditional credit process. The characteristics of the sought objectives require the implementation of two further phases compared with the traditional process, one at the beginning and one at the end (Figure 6.2), which characterize the socio-ethical aims of microfinance and the ultimate objective of the effective and lasting development of the beneficiary.

Some operational and management characteristics depend on the supplying institution and on the type of programme being considered. MFIs, which fund their activities mainly through deposits and are based on balance principles between saving and lending activities, direct the management and the operations towards aspects such as the quality of the lending portfolio and the level of risk exposure. They also balance risks and returns, by achieving through an adequate level of operating efficiency.

On the other hand, MFIs operating with public grants and soft loans prefer the outreach objectives rather than financial performance goals, which represent compulsory restrictions. Below Figure 6.2 shows the differences between the traditional credit process and the microcredit process. The two processes differ in the initial and the final phases. The other phases are identical even if they are characterized by differing operating methods and by the use of specific instruments. Such difference is

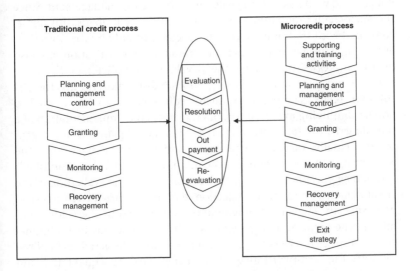

Figure 6.2 Traditional credit process vs. microcredit process

more evident in the sub-phases relative to credit granting, especially for the evaluation.

Supporting and training activities: this phase is one of the features of microcredit processes, which points out the focus on socio-ethical and beneficiaries' development objectives. Generally, especially regarding microfinance included in development cooperation programmes, MFIs are assisted by other partners that supply training services, social services and other activities implying a specific knowledge of the territory and the target beneficiary. Socio-ethical goals imply that the involved MFIs take particular care of the phase preceding the microcredit supply; in fact, the study of the local context, of its particular needs and of the economical situation in which the institutions will operate, require preliminary training activities. These activities are finalized to root a credit culture among the future beneficiaries and local operators, in order to favour the success of the programme; such particular activities are unfamiliar to the traditional credit. The traditional financial intermediaries that take part in microcredit programmes generally entrust to MFIs all the activities, as the one described above, that require a good territorial knowledge.

Planning and management control: in this phase, which belongs to the traditional credit process, all the activities related to the organization of the credit production and distribution is performed. These activities have to be coherent with the pursued objectives, with the development policies and with risk–return goals agreed by the top management. Since the microcredit programmes often use grants and soft loans, this phase, compared with traditional credit, is affected not only by the objectives and the operational requirements of the supplying institution, but also by the strategies defined by the development policies of the large national and international donors. Another distinction regards the distribution phase. The nature of microcredit, especially when offered to populations living in rural areas, often requires the implementation of a travelling distribution network that needs a careful planning and organization. Finally, during the planning and management control, the accounting software system and the monitoring system are established.

Granting: this phase refers to the acquisition and the evaluation of the credit requests. The approval/rejection resolution is provided by a special body that, in microcredit programmes, is identified in the credit committee. The granting phase includes four sub-phases, as in traditional credit process. The *evaluation* is the combination of the activities finalized to verify the creditworthiness of the beneficiary. The qualitative and quantitative features of the borrower are evaluated in both historical

and prospective terms, by the gathering of the client's relevant information. In microcredit programmes this activity is generally carried out by loan officers by means of interviews and visits to the potential beneficiary. The loan officers assist the future beneficiary in filling in the credit application; then, the loan officers formulate a personal opinion which will influence the credit committee in the credit resolution. *Resolution, out-payment* and *re-evaluation* follow the same principles of traditional finance. In development cooperation programmes, the credit out-payment can be entrusted to a third party, most of the times a local partner.

Monitoring: this phase includes all the activities necessary to the control of the credit cash flow concerning the on-time repayments, and the prompt management of default positions. Such management depends on the ability to anticipate the occurrence of the default, by means of adequate accounting and daily monitoring. It is, therefore, necessary to have a reporting and management information system among all organizational levels. In microcredit, particular attention is dedicated to the positions regarding solidarity groups, since the multiplier effect of any possible default could represent a high risk. Hence, the information regarding these 'groups' should be constantly updated. When the credit is assisted by physical collateral – usually the property of the beneficiary and his family (television, fridge, etc.) – the loan officer will have to check on their condition during his visits.

Recovery management: this phase concerns certified default positions that cannot be recovered. In this case, the local legislation of the target territory plays an essential role: the chances of recovery are, in fact, tied to the presence and the intervention of external bodies, such as tribunal jurisdictions.

Exit strategy is the other distinctive phase of microcredit programmes, in particular those included in development cooperation programmes. It refers to the exit strategy at the end of the programme. In fact, in the exit phase, the supplying institution must ensure that the funds dedicated to microcredit have generated enough returns to guarantee the continuity of the supported activities after the conclusion of the microcredit programme and the exit of the MFI. In this phase, the socio-ethical objective becomes significantly important. The microcredit must trigger a virtuous mechanism and promote sustainable economical cycles over time and not only during the programme. For this phase, for example, the destination and the function of the residual rotation fund must be programmed; the opening of a working 'service point' with specific operating staff can be planned; alternative funding must be provided. This new scenario represents the final objective of the programme in terms of future sustainability.

6.5 Process-related risks

Chapter 5 analyses the typologies of risk that can occur in the typical activities of microfinance. In this section, the operational risks regarding MFIs are analysed in greater detail. In order to do so, we will consider operational risks without making a distinction between the different typologies of institutions. In fact, the MFI's complexity, its dimensions, its particular equipment of human and material resources, can vary the incidence of risks but not their occurrence.

The occurrence of operational risks regards the whole universe of MFIs; the effects are inevitably negative for all institutions. As the risk management concerns the complexity of the intermediary, either operational risks or financial risks must have an appropriate consideration in the MFIs' policies. The aim of an integrated management is to quantify the overall risks in order to maximize the returns and the value of the institution. Therefore, from a risk management point of view, it becomes necessary for all MFIs to consider the operational risk management an essential phase.

Operational risk is defined as the risk of loss resulting from inadequate or failed internal processes, people and systems or from external events (see Chapter 5). The occurrence of these risks depends on the circumstance that the processes related to the production activities (section 6.3) have not been clearly defined and, as a consequence, are not managed correctly by the responsible functions. This inevitably affects the achievement of the objectives and, therefore, the satisfaction of the client's needs. Furthermore, in taking these risks MFIs could undergo losses, fraud or abuses that have manifested themselves frequently in the MFIs' operations.

The risk management process comprises three main phases: *identification, measurement and monitoring, quantification and management* of the risks linked to the single processes. This process of identification, measuring and control must be implemented for each MFI's process; consequently, the internal control system must be enabled on each one of those processes. In this sense the task of management is, first of all, to identify the *key variables* for the monitoring of risks; the second step concerns fixing *early warning or alert limits* for those risks thought to be strategic in relation to the monitored activities. Obviously this process will differ, according to the nature of the institution and to the considered type of microcredit programme, in relation to how important the risks are in order to achieve the MFIs' objectives.

The risk management process is linked to the control process and is incorporated into it. The trend regarding the financial intermediaries' policies tends to consider the risk management process as a part of the internal control system to enhance the institutional governance. Risk management and control process have deep connections; the control must be a part of the daily operations of the MFI in order to manage the risks. At least one *risk management function* is suitable for more structured MFIs, semi-formal and formal; this function must continuously guarantee the identification, measurement and quantification of the risk. The identification of processes and risks is essential for a good control system. The operational risks that mainly affect MFIs are:

- compliance risk;
- interest conflict risk;
- risk resulting from inadequate or failed internal processes;
- risk resulting from people;
- risk resulting from the fraud of the top or middle management;
- risk of theft and internal fraud or unauthorized activities;
- reputational risk;
- risk of compensation, benefit and termination issue;
- risk of losses arising from disruption of business or system failures;
- risk of key performance indicators;
- risk of losses arising from errors in the budgeting process;
- risk of losses arising from errors in the strategic process.

The *compliance risk* consists in the possibility that the processes implemented are not compliant to the procedures of the MFI; this risk can arise from a mistaken definition of the process, from a poor functioning of operating units or from human error. The *interest conflict risk* is represented by the possibility, in the operations, of a co-mingling of individual, MFI's and clients' interests. The *risk resulting from inadequate or failed internal process* is represented by the possibility that the MFI's internal processes do not guarantee the achievement of the objectives for which they were drawn up and/or require costs that are greater than budgeted and sustainable costs. The *risk resulting from people* is the possibility that human resources engaged in the management and/or control of a process do not have the skills, experience or the professional requirements needed to ensure the achievement of the expected objectives or to reduce the main related risks to acceptable levels. Within the sphere of risks concerning human resources, the *risk resulting from the fraud of top or middle management* assumes particular relevance. It consists in the possibility

that the management staff can change documents (i.e.; budgets, reports, statements) with the intention of deceiving the recipients of the information, for example, the donors. Moreover, the *risk of theft and internal fraud* is the possibility that the employees, whether alone or in collusion with third parties, perpetrate fraud, theft or carry out unauthorized activities against the MFI or the beneficiaries; it could happen, for example, in terms of unauthorized utilization of financial and non-financial assets. Loan officers' frauds are the highest operational risk for MFIs.

The *reputational risk* is the possibility that the MFI damages its relationship with clients, suppliers, donors and can lose professional employees, harming its image in the marketplace. This risk is associated with the stakeholders' perception on the respectability and professional integrity of the MFI and its employees, on the technical and professional skills of all the resources in managing its business and on the quality and level of the products and services offered. Within reputational risk, for MFIs particular importance is assumed by the *risk related to the customer satisfaction* that is linked to outreach goals and occurs when the processes are not drawn up in such a way as to meet the expectations of the beneficiaries; for example when the evaluation process is too articulated, or when the MFI is unable to offer the client responsive product and services. The *risk related to communication* is another kind of reputational risk represented by the possibility that the communication system – vertical (top-down and bottom-up) or horizontal – is ineffective. For example, the employees are not fully aware of the mission, the objectives and the strategies of the MFI; the management does not receive adequate information on the organizational staff, especially local operating units and loan officers, and, therefore, it cannot intervene to rectify any eventual inefficiencies; the employees do not have the necessary support to fulfil their obligations or to act in the presence of technical and operational problems.

The *risk of compensation, benefit and termination issue* is represented by the possibility that the employees do not agree with the performance indicators used by the MFI. This may imply that the employees, in order to reach the performance level and attain the incentive, are tempted to act in a manner that does not conform to business objectives or to strategies and ethical standards of the MFI. The incentive system is still an unresolved problem for many MFIs and it is the major cause of fraud and theft, especially by loan officers. The *risk of losses arising from disruption of business or system* concerns the possibility that the used information system may be inadequate for the operational processes

and does not satisfy the operating needs, compromising the reliability of data and information. The *risk of key performance indicators* concerns the possibility that the used indicators are inadequate for representing the true financial and economical situation of the MFI. It can happen when the performance indicators are not correctly balanced (for example, between financial indicators and sustainability and outreach indicators); or performance indicators do not consider the relationship between the long-term returns and the objectives and strategies of the project.

Related to the financial management is the *risk of losses arising from errors in budgeting process*, that is, the possibility that the defined objectives are not attainable and not agreed upon. Finally, it is necessary to mention the *risk arising from errors in the strategic process*. In this context, the risk emerges when the MFI does not point out and analyse the information concerning the target group, or when it disregards the regulatory framework and the real possibilities of development that the environment actually offers.

6.6   Control typologies

In order to draw up an efficient internal control system it is necessary to consider both the organizational structure and the process elements. MFIs have different organizational structures depending on the institutional typology; consequently the typology, the bodies and the processes of control must suit the structural and organizational characteristics of the concerned institution. In fact, the control components depend on the activities and processes that are carried out, as well as on the objectives pursued, and on the human and financial resources available.

Control activities are functional to the operations, to the related risks and to the environment in which the MFI operates. The internal control system aims to guarantee and monitor the effectiveness and efficiency of the operational processes. This requires the reliability and integrity of the accounting and management information, both for the MFI's internal use – such as operations and management needs – and for external requirements – such as the compliance to local law and supervision regulation.

An effective control system requires dedicated human and financial resources. The simple structure of some MFIs is combined with the need to implement an effective system that defines the control activity and attributes the relative responsibility to the appropriate bodies. Then, all MFIs must implement an internal control system that respects the general principles – functional to the system effectiveness – of separation between management and control activities to avoid interest conflict risks. Once

the MFIs' processes, the responsible functions and the related risk typologies have been identified, the internal control system is planned and the methodologies to manage the identified risks are defined. In this planning phase, the strategic objectives are taken into consideration and, therefore, it is decided what level of risk protection is necessary and which control typology must be implemented.

The control structure often does not correspond to the optimum model, but simply to the most suitable one for the specific situation, for the frame of reference and for the risk-return objectives that characterize the MFI. The control system allows the management to handle all kinds of risk, reducing their consequent negative impact as well as preventing them from arising, in order to allow the achievement of risk and performance. In this way, the internal control system is a governance instrument of the institution, since it allows to promptly correct any malfunctions and to achieve effectively and efficiently the MFI's objectives.

The information management system, on the other hand, provides a decision-making support to the various bodies of the organizational structure, allowing the correct management of the processes. The need to monitor and control the MFI's operations implies the coordination between control and executive bodies and the implementation of an adequate reporting system to the top management. This system allows to constantly monitor the level of risks and the staff members involved in the operating functions. The control typologies on the activities and on the human resources depend on the specific MFI; the control activity requires the use of different control instruments (Table 6.1).

Table 6.1 Control typology – control instruments

Control typology	Control instruments
Operational control	• Manuals • Instructions • Procedures • Financial delegation of powers
Inspection control	• On-site inspection reports
Management control	• Strategic planning • Annual budgeting • Portfolio situation • Accounting and financial reporting
Quality control	• Mission • Ethical code
Reporting control	• Internal controls: check lists and reports • External controls: balance statement and documents for disclosure requirements

Operational controls are carried out by operating units (for example by loan officer) during their activities; included in this typology are the controls deriving from the implementation of operating instructions contained in the operating manuals (for example, the credit manual) and in the operating procedures. Also included in this typology are the automatic software controls; it happens, for example, in the evaluation and in the granting of credit, when the staff member exceeds the agreed limits.

Inspection controls on the operating units, both front and back office, are aimed at verifying the compliance of operations with internal and external regulations. Inspection controls are advisable even for the simplest MFIs, in order to prevent the fraud risk, the compliance risk and the risk resulting from inadequate or failed internal processes (see section 6.5).

Management controls on accounting documents such as budgets, statements, credit portfolios, etc., aim to verify the MFI's situation in its capital, economical and financial components.

Quality controls on socio-ethical activities are implemented to verify the quality of the offered services.

Reporting controls refer to internal communication of the MFIs and to disclosure requirements.

The control procedures must be described in appropriate documents (procedures, manuals, operating instructions), containing clear and defined rules on control activities and responsibilities. These documents must contain the description of the instruments to be used and the information flow that must be provided to manage all the risk typologies, in order to guarantee continuously a correct operations and a flow of reports on the obtained results and on the risks.

An MFI's internal control system could be structured as are the ones used by other financial intermediaries, according to the following three levels:

- *First level* These controls ensure that activities are compliant to procedures and manuals; they are carried out by the same operating units (for example, hierarchical controls), or incorporated into the software procedures, or performed by the back-office functions.
- *Second level* These consist in risk management controls, which aim to concur in the definition of the risk measurement system, to verify that the limits assigned to the operative functions are respected and to control the coherence of the operations of the single production areas with the assigned risk–return objectives. These controls require a specific risk management function.

- *Third level* These controls consist in the internal auditing process and aim to identify anomalies, violations of procedures and internal rules; they also evaluate that the overall internal control system works correctly.

This monitoring activity can be carried out continuously, periodically or exceptionally, also by means of on-site inspections. The control bodies must be independent from the operating units.

6.7 The incentive system

The incentive systems used by MFIs can provide a positive contribution in order to achieve the productivity goals. These are also indirect instruments for the achievement of outreach and sustainability goals. On the other hand, if used in an improper way, the incentive system represents a source of operational risk for MFIs, and, as such, it has to be controlled.

MFIs' experiences in using these systems suggest that, at present, there is not an ideal model of incentive scheme. In some cases, the negative side effects are higher than the benefits and the system has led to an increase of the risk of theft and internal fraud or unauthorized activities. Hence, it is necessary to perform a careful monitoring that focuses on the human resources which, inside the MFI, can be interested in the incentive system, and also analyses all the levels of the organizational pyramid that can represent a source of risk.

Why is the incentive system so important in microfinance activities? Because MFIs are characterized by high-intensity human labour activities that imply higher responsibilities than the traditional banking system does. In microfinance, incentives are used at all levels of the institutional pyramid, including clients, staff members, management, up to the board of directors (Table 6.2). The achieved results by the incentive system for

Table 6.2 Matrix incentives/beneficiaries

Institutional pyramid levels	Intangible incentives	Tangible non-monetary incentives	Tangible monetary incentives
Board of directors	X	X	X
Management	X	X	X
Loan officer	X	X	X
Clients		X	X

clients are mainly positive; in many successful microcredit projects, many mechanisms have been used to induce on-time repayment by the borrowers. For example, among the most used ones, there are *graduation principles* through which the so-called excellent debtors are offered larger loan amounts and longer loan terms; another interesting instrument is the *interest rebate*, which consists in reducing the interest rate. The aim of these instruments is to encourage the clients to adopt correct behaviour with the MFI (a timely repayment activity allows the MFI to be sustainable in the long term), but also to gain their loyalty.

At the second level of the institutional pyramid there is the operating staff. Staff expenses are undoubtedly the most important category of costs, considering also the remote areas in which they operate. The staff has a wider discretion compared with a bank's personnel. The compensation and the performance measurement systems assume a strategic importance, with a great impact on MFIs. Incentives are relevant in any activity, but the best application has been found with loan officers and lending operations staff involved in microcredit projects. This typology of operators plays a crucial role: they generate and safeguard the majority of the assets, determining most of the income of microfinance organizations. Therefore, incentives have to be adapted to performance. In the case of loan officers, the incentive system sometimes may result in contrast to sustainability and outreach goals. For example, an incentive system that rewards the loan officer in proportion to the number of stipulated contracts may compromise the programme's sustainability inducing the loan officer to stipulate microcredit contracts also with beneficiaries without the necessary reliability requirements.

Another important use of incentives is finalized to make the MFI's human resources loyal; the costs of searching, selecting and training new resources would be, in most occasions, significantly higher than the incentive itself. In such context, the incentive system can really help to provide higher personnel stability which, because of the nature and the location of the programmes, is obviously low.

The higher levels of the institutional pyramid are also included in the incentive systems. If, on one hand, the board of directors aims to be rewarded in terms of image, which is well in line with the pursued objectives, on the other hand, the monetary incentives remain important. Monetary incentives surely have a great impact on the rewarded resources, but, at a second stage, other types of incentive, such as personal ones, arise (Holtmann et al., 2002), (Table 6.3).

Table 6.3   Typologies of incentives

Intangible incentives	• Sense of mission • Job satisfaction • Possibilities for promotion
Tangible non-monetary incentives	• Non-monetary benefits
Tangible monetary incentives	• Monetary bonus systems • Profit sharing • Stock ownership

6.8   Conclusion

Is it possible to define a standard internal control system that suits all MFIs? The answer to this question is surely no. The main reasons are essentially two. The first concerns the vast typology of microfinance institutions; the second concerns the diversity of the specific objectives of each considered project or programme.

The microcredit projects included in development cooperation programmes, as well as other microfinance programmes, need effective information systems that allow for controlling the execution of operational activities at all organization levels. However, for microcredit programmes included in development cooperation programmes, the socio-ethical elements and the typology of funding (usually donations) imply that the process elements normally monitored by traditional financial intermediaries become relatively less important than the outreach objective. Anyhow, also in these circumstances it is important that the typical financial process contains the minimum elements of operational and management control, as well as an adequate reporting, especially for donors. In this perspective, MFIs and donors have to work in order to improve the quality of the internal control systems adopted so far.

In the other microfinance projects the situation is different. MFIs, without being traditional financial intermediaries, carry out activities very similar to those performed by commercial banks, but include specific features that depend on the specific target typology and on the offered product. For these MFIs it is necessary to have a structured internal control system that considers the specific risks and allows a constant monitoring. Such system will be different for the specific MFI and will depend on the typology of the supplied products, because the variables that are considered strategic for control will change.

Finally, the incentive system can be a useful instrument to achieve the performance, sustainability and outreach objectives only if adequately structured. In fact, the incentive system can imply phenomena such as adverse selection and the risk of theft and internal fraud or unauthorized activities. For such reasons, these mechanisms must be used in an accurate way and under an effective and efficient internal control system.

7
Microfinance Performance

Marco Tutino

7.1 Introduction

This chapter proposes a model of performance analysis for microfinance programmes and institutions in order to evaluate actual or expected results. In particular, performance evaluation approach should be considered from two distinct perspectives:

1) the first approach is related to the performance of a single project managed adopting a perspective like that of project financing, as could occur in the case of a non-formal institution, mainly an NGO of reduced dimensions;
2) the other performance evaluation relates to an MFI that handles significant operative volumes, and reasons from the vantage point of a portfolio of projects.

The theoretical framework, consisting of the traditional literature on performance, is contextualized according to the specific rationale that characterizes the microfinance operation. Performance evaluation, moreover, is not a new subject matter in microfinance. On the international level, different models of evaluation have been developed over the course of the last few years. This chapter presents a brief reconstruction of the methodologies currently used in microfinance for performance analysis, identifying the main characteristics of each, the areas of analysis considered by their measure, and the principal limitations on information that can occur.

Aside from these, the chapter proposes an alternative performance measure for microfinance. The innovative force is inspired with respect

to three specific requirements: the first is the strict derivation of the classical doctrine on performance analysis – that assures the rigorousness and reliability; its adaptability to formal and informal institutions, including non-profit organizations that are less formal and complex; and the need to find a correct balance between the two dichotomous objectives that characterize microfinance, that is, sustainability and outreach.

7.2 Performance analysis

7.2.1 Performance features

Performance analysis is the process of evaluating the actual results produced by a project, or by an institution, in relation to the results that were expected. Because the processes and activities that make up the project or the institution are diverse, they should be analysed in relation to the distinct areas of management to which they belong. Therefore, the foundation of performance evaluation is the availability of data relative to each area of management and to the individual operations of each area, which form a system of indicators that offers adequate information on the whole. Performance evaluation is a process based on complementary, yet diverse, information related to the operation of singular aspects of management, and it is conditioned by the necessity to arrange the information so that, even if it is a synopsis, it permits us to satisfy three main objectives:

- to formulate *ex ante* realistic expectations of the available resources;
- to monitor *over time* the management's operational ability to achieve the objectives;
- to evaluate *ex post* the results achieved.

Performance sustainability over time and the achievement of objectives are based also on a process of data collection, classification, selection and organization of data. This analysis, and presentation of the information used, allows for the real time correction of eventual distortions, which cause deviation from the fixed objectives.[1]

The data collection, classification and selection process must consider information relevant for the ongoing monitoring of the processes and activities of each area of the operation that influences the evaluation of the performance as a whole: the act of data collection, classification and selection of data are, thus, conditions necessary for their elaboration and successive presentation as relevant information. The presentation of the information collected acquires an immediate, indicative/signpost

value when it is reorganized in quantitative or qualitative indicators. *A performance evaluation model, therefore, can be defined as a coordinated system of processing information, which allows to evaluate each operations of the entity – be it a project or an institution – by the use of indicators.*

In order to understand the diverse perspectives and methodologies of analysing performance, as well as the complexity of management of a project or of an institution, the indicators of the evaluation system adopted for each area of analysis should be considered individually. This individual consideration responds to the need to analyse each operational area in relation to the different weight, or importance, assigned to the task in respect to the overall performance.

An efficient system of evaluation must have the requisite characteristics for achieving the following objectives:

- the comparability of performance *in time*;
- the comparability of performance *in space*;
- the comparability of performance *with respect to a benchmark*.

The comparability of performance over time identifies how well internal management can monitor the operations of the entity by accessing a constant flow of relevant information: continued monitoring allows intervention and timely decision-making in order to avoid negative results that would influence the overall performance. The comparability of performance in space, however, is a necessary condition for informing, those other than internal management, even those who intend to compare periodic results of a project/institution with results of other projects or other institutions: the different degree of success with respect to a comparable initiative allows the evaluation of the efficacy and efficiency in terms of resources employed. In this respect, performance analysis is an important instrument for investors in decision-making. As for the comparability of results with respect to an industry benchmark, the possibility of comparing the results produced and measured with an integrated system of indicators recognized as an industry standard of performance allows a qualitative–quantitative comparison of results achieved (*actual performance*) with respect to the desired result to satisfy sustainability over time (*benchmark performance*). From this perspective, performance analysis is also a useful instrument for policy makers.

7.2.2   Microfinance performance

From an economic-business perspective, the concept of performance is strictly tied to the earnings of the business (net profit), which is understood to be the difference – positive or negative – derived from the

netting of the proceeds produced by activities and the costs sustained for those activities computed on an accrual basis. The perspective of profit generation has, thus, focused the analysis of the performance in terms of profitability and in terms of technical, operational and strategic efficiency of the business.

Differently from a profit-oriented business, the parameter of profit maximization, widely accepted in competitive market-analysis, faces an obstacle in the world of microfinance: outreach. If, on one hand, the conditions for achieving economic-financial balance in the initiative must be respected in order to guarantee its sustainability in the long term, then, on the other hand, owing to the complex dichotomy of the fundamental goals involved, the fundamental objectives of microfinance cannot be achieved adopting the same performance indicators system currently used in capital markets. While in capital markets the degree of success of an initiative is accurately measured with indicators that signal whether the earnings expectations have been met, from a microfinance perspective the system of indicators must be integrated, and at times corrected, in order to take into consideration that:

- specific objectives of a microfinance activity (like outreach) and the degree of success is measured considering parameters different from that of earnings alone (for example, ethical-solidarity guidelines);
- the benchmark can always differ depending on the specific outreach goals of the financed project.[2]

Thus, in accordance with the type of intervention required as per development politics and social and humanitarian objectives, and once the sphere of influence of the project is defined, it is also necessary to have a viable calculation that can evaluate results on the basis of a double binomial interpretation:

- the *economic-financial sustainability* of the projects and institutions in order to guarantee the regeneration of resources at the base of the microfinance process;
- the *satisfaction of institutional objectives*, reviving the concept of outreach.

With respect to the above-mentioned parameters, it is necessary to define a system of performance indicators that satisfy at least two objectives:

- offering efficient information to the stakeholders in the microfinance sector (donors, investors, MFIs and customers);

- considering the characteristics of a cycle of financing that is different, if not alternative, from the traditional cycle.

In synthesis, from a microfinance perspective, compared with that of a purely performance based analysis of the business, the main characteristics of performance analysis should consider that:

- there is a *trade-off* between the satisfaction of the *development goals* in the particular area of the intervention (with regard to the number and quality of the beneficiaries of microfinance – or outreach) and with the goals of *economic-financial sustainability* of the project/MFI;
- there is a *different quality of benchmark* for measuring the degree of fulfilment of the goals of the financed projects/MFIs using a methodology tailored to the informational needs of microfinance, not only in terms of profit produced but also in ethical-solidarity objectives achieved.

Thus, because of the different meaning of performance with regard to microfinance, it becomes necessary to adapt the traditional model of performance evaluation – partially redefining or adapting, using corrective mechanisms and all the associated instruments used in traditional analysis – in order to account for different objectives in respect to maximization of profit.

7.3   Performance evaluation model for microfinance project

Despite a lot of attention being given to the evolutionary dynamics of microfinance business, not much consideration has been dedicated to an analysis of microfinance in terms of monitoring and evaluating single projects. This is particularly relevant in the case of informal and semi-formal MFIs promoting a few microfinance programmes a year, thanks to public and private donations.

Adjusting the focus of performance analysis to a project financing approach (and not to the overall performance of an MFI), the following objectives should be achieved:

- a valuation approach adapted from the traditional performance analysis model consistent with the accounting practices followed by non-formal and semi-formal MFIs;
- a set of project indicators specifically tailored to the non-formal and semi-formal MFIs' financial statement.

A performance analysis of a single project should at least consider the following areas:

- management analysis;
- cash flow analysis;
- earnings analysis;
- portfolio quality analysis;
- outreach analysis;
- subsidies dependence analysis.

Management analysis

The indicators for the analysis and monitoring of the management area should analyse at least:

- the cost composition;
- the productivity of the personnel employed.

Productivity and efficiency ratios can be restricted to cost composition and productivity of the personnel. The analysis of the project's productivity is geared towards an evaluation of the composition of the main costs of the project, mainly personnel, consulting and training costs (Box 7.1). The analysis of the productivity of the personnel should focus on the productivity of the loan officers 'because they are the primary generators of revenue' and on all of the personnel.[3] The recourse to external auditing must be evaluated in light of the number of personnel employed in the project (Box 7.2).

Box 7.1   Cost composition indicators

7.1.1   Cost of personnel/Total current cost
7.1.2   Consulting costs/Total current cost
7.1.3   Cost of training/Total current cost

Box 7.2   Personnel productivity indicators

7.2.1   Personnel productivity

a. Consulting costs/Number of personnel
b. Number of active borrowers/Number of personnel

7.2.2   Loan officer productivity

Number of active borrowers/Number of loan officers

7.2.3   Personnel allocation

Number of loan officers/Number of personnel

Cash flow analysis

Performance indicators of financial analysis should be computed in relation to different areas. However, in order to avoid a large number of indicators, it is possible to limit the analysis to two specific dimensions:

- net cash flow generated by the whole project;
- net cash flow generated by the outstanding portfolio connected with the microcredit activity.

These ratios are suggested in order to measure the capability of the project to generate positive net financial flows (Box 7.3). With regard to project evaluation, it could be useful to focus on the microcredit activity, especially in those cases where microcredit represents the main component of the initiative.

Earnings analysis

The earnings analysis is limited to reviewing revenues and costs connected to microcredit that are relative to the disbursement and reimbursement of funds, and other microfinance activities, such as financial services provided to the beneficiaries, producing interest income and active fees for the project (Box 7.4).

Portfolio quality analysis

Portfolio quality analysis is relevant because microcredit activity is the main profit-generating area in a microfinance programme. The set of indicators should provide information on the percentage of *non-performing*

Box 7.3   Cash flow indicators

7.3.1   Net cash flow generated by the whole project

Cash inflow of the project in the period – Cash outflow of the project in the period

7.3.2   Net cash flow generated by the outstanding portfolio

Cash inflow of the microcredit activity in the period – Cash outflow of the microcredit activity in the period

---

Box 7.4   Portfolio profitability indicators

7.4.1   Interest income/Average portfolio
7.4.2   Interest income + fees/Average portfolio

loans, on the *guarantees* and *loan loss reserves* available, on the effective *losses to be written off* (Box 7.5).

Box 7.5 Portfolio quality indicators

7.5.1 Arrears rate

Amount in arrears/Portfolio outstanding (including amounts past due)[4]

7.5.2 Portfolio at risk

Outstanding balance of loans with payments past due/Portfolio outstanding (including amounts past due)

7.5.3 Delinquent borrower

Number of delinquent borrowers/Total number of active borrowers

7.5.4 Repayment rate

Amount received (including prepayments and past due amounts)/Amount due (excluding past due amounts)

7.5.5 Loan loss ratio

Amount written off in the period/Average portfolio outstanding for the period

7.5.6 Loan collateral ratio

Collaterals/Portfolio outstanding

7.5.7 Loan loss reserve ratio

Loan loss reserve for the period/Portfolio outstanding for the period

---

Outreach analysis

We have seen in Chapter 4 that the aim of microfinance programmes, which is linked to the fight against financial exclusion and extreme poverty, is easily classified as ethical, and it is strictly related to outreach goals. Thus, it could be useful for donors and microfinance practitioners to consider outreach indicators while evaluating the overall performance (Box 7.6). In this case, outreach indicators should consider both dimensions of breadth and depth.

Box 7.6 Outreach indicators

7.6.1 Number of beneficiaries/Total portfolio outstanding
7.6.2 Number of women/Number of beneficiaries
7.6.3 Average loan amount/GNP per capita
7.6.4 Number of beneficiaries under poverty line/Number of beneficiaries

---

Subsidies dependence analysis

The capacity to operate independently from subsidies can be taken as a proxy for the sustainability of the project. In particular, it is worth considering both the dependence ratio on in-kind subsidies and on financial subsidies (Box 7.7). In fact, subsidies of this type are usually supplied in two distinct ways: *in-money subsidies*, in the form of financial participation in the project and by *in-kind subsidies*, in term of technical services and infrastructures provided.[5] In summary, even if the traditional approach to MFI evaluation is the dominant viewpoint of performance analysis, the performance evaluation of individual projects allows one to deepen the analysis to microfinance programmes carried out by informal and semi-formal MFIs, and which are the basis of the success of the microfinance market as a whole.

Box 7.7 Subsidies dependence indicators

7.7.1   In-kind subsidies/Total current costs
7.7.2   Financial subsidies received/Total funds of the project

---

7.4   Performance evaluation models for MFIs

The management features of microfinance institutions, in particular with regard to the characteristics of the beneficiaries served and the products requested, as well as the process for distribution of credit, create two requirements related to the selection of a system of performance indicators:

- the need for monitoring traditional aspects of management typical of all financial institutions;
- the need to consider the influence of certain instruments and forms of financing which sustain microfinance activities in order to compare different types of institutions.

The adequacy of the system of indicators is a necessary condition for the performance analysis that can be conducted with a different width and depth according to the aspects observed and the analytical level and completeness of the requested information. In order to be considered adequate, the system of indicators must possess certain specific characteristics:

- *simplicity*: the indicators should be as easy to measure and implement as possible;

- *relevance*: the indicators should measure aspects of projects that are of particular interest and importance;
- *uniqueness*: within the set of indicators, another indicator must add significant additional information that is noteworthy or of value;
- *completeness*: to the extent possible, the set of indicators should collectively measure all the major aspects of projects.[6]

During the 1990s, there was a growing interest on the part of financial institutions in microfinance. As a result, several performance evaluation indicators emerged in relation to different areas of management considered as the most important in evaluating performance for MFIs. The results achieved were diverse. In actuality, some models of evaluation were generally accepted and have been currently adopted by institutions to monitor and evaluate the business. Each of these models focused on specific profiles of analysis (Box 7.8). These models contribute to raising the level of informative transparency with regard to the processes of credit

---

Box 7.8 Most common models of performance evaluation for MFIs

PEARLS Model (1990) from the World Council of Credit Unions. Protection acronym, Effective financial structure, Asset quality, Rates of return and costs, Liquidity and Signs of growth, it is a system of 39 indicators used for monitoring performance of a specific type of microfinance institution: credit unions.

CAMEL Model (1993) from Accion International. Capital adequacy acronym, Asset quality, Management, Earnings and Liquidity management, it is a system of 21 indicators currently utilized by North American banks to evaluate performance, focusing principally on the financial aspects of management.

GIRAFE Model (1999) from Planet Rating. Governance and decision-making processes acronym. Information and management tools, Risk analysis and control, Activities and loan portfolio, Funding: equity and liabilities, Efficiency and liability. It is an instrument of quantitative and qualitative evaluation of performance and of the risks borne by the MFI. The qualitative analysis focuses on the success of the strategy verifying the quality of the management processes and the efficiency of the information system with the objective of guaranteeing the internal control functions.

CGAP Model from the Consultative Group to Assist the Poorest and the Inter-American Development Bank measures performance utilizing qualitative and quantitative indicators. The performance indicators are concentrated on the four areas of analysis: institutional factors, services/markets/clients, objective strategies and financial performance.

<www.mip.org/pubs/mbp/camel.htm; http://www.accion.org/>
<http://www.calmeadow.com/metrofund.htm; http://www.cgap.org/>
<http://www.mixmarket.org/>.

management of MFIs. They have solved the questions about terminology and composition of the accounting items in order to better monitoring and evaluating performance of microfinance institutions.[7] Nevertheless, these models are not completely in agreement in terms of areas analysed, and on which to concentrate the evaluation of performance.

The logic of construction of a performance evaluation system is in part undermined by the numerous indicators identified in the more popular models for performance evaluation in the field of microfinance. This has in turn caused a loss of significance of the classification criteria of the same indicators formerly adopted for the distinct profiles of analysis of the MFIs. Our model, adopting a traditional approach to performance evaluation for financial intermediaries, requires the organization of selected indicators according to the following characteristic areas of analysis:

- *Management area*, including indicators of productivity, operational efficiency and of the portfolio quality;
- *Profitability area*, including indicators of portfolio, total assets and equity profitability;
- *Sustainability area*, including indicators of operational self-sufficiency and fully-financial self-sufficiency;
- *Leverage and financial structure area*, including ratios to indicate qualitative-quantitative structure on the sources of funds.

The model also provides accounting adjustments to financial statement of MFIs according to:

- comparability of the performance in time and in space;
- the influence of subsidies on the MFIs balance sheet, which can modify the informational values of the indicators.

7.4.1   Performance indicators of management area

The management area of an MFI can be analysed considering three distinct profiles:

- the productivity of the personnel employed;
- the efficiency of the operating structure in relation to the loan portfolio;
- the quality of the loan portfolio (outstanding loans).

The productivity of the personnel employed

The productivity of the personnel can be measured by comparing specific variables: the number of employees; the number of loan officers; the number of outstanding deposits; the number of active borrowers and

---

Box 7.9   Personnel productivity indicators

7.9.1   Personnel productivity
Number of active borrowers / Number of personnel

7.9.2   Loan officer productivity
Number of active borrowers / Number of loan officers

7.9.3   Personnel allocation ratio
Number of loan officers / Number of personnel

---

the number of the active depositors (Box 7.9). The productivity of the personnel employed is traditionally measured with the indicator 7.9.1.[8] Comparing the number of active borrowers with the total number of personnel employed will offer a summary measure of the overall productivity. However, because only a small part of the overall personnel is working directly in the credit activity (generally as loan officers), it is usually a good idea to provide further information such as that offered by indicator 7.9.2. Because the indicators presented do not allow for a valuation of the composition of the personnel, and in particular the resources directly dedicated to the credit process, indicator 7.9.3 can result as a useful measure.

The efficiency of the operating structure

In financial intermediaries, operating efficiency is measured by comparing the costs in relation to the loan portfolio. In particular, the indicators currently utilized are comparing accounting configurations of cost with the average gross loan portfolio. The reason for using the average gross loan portfolio, rather than the gross loan portfolio, lies in the fact that within a set period the value of the loan portfolio changes in relation to the amount of loans disbursed and those that have been repaid. Thus, one should use the average value of outstanding loans, which should allow for efficiency indicators to not be influenced by the normal peaks and valleys of that activity.

The accounting items that summarily express the most often used cost configuration are:

- operating expenses, which indicate the total operating costs;
- personnel expenses, that is, the part of the operating costs absorbed by the personnel employed;
- administrative expenses, that is, the part of the operating costs absorbed by administrative expenses.

Box 7.10   Operating efficiency indicators

7.10.1   Adjusted operating expenses/Loan portfolio

(Operating expenses + in-kind donations)/Average gross loan portfolio

7.10.2   Adjusted personnel expenses/Loan portfolio

(Personnel expense + in-kind donations for personnel)/Average gross loan portfolio

7.10.3   Adjusted administrative expenses/Loan portfolio

(Administrative expenses + in-kind donations)/Average gross loan portfolio

7.10.4   Cost per borrower

(Operating   expenses + in-kind   donations)/Average   number   of   active borrowers

---

In order to construct the efficiency indicators, nonetheless, it is necessary to consider the presence of subsidies provided to the MFIs as in-kind donations. The reason is that the MFI would not be able to cover operating costs, in the long term, without the support of in-kind donations. That is, it could be that the MFI is in reality operating at a loss. Thus, considering in-kind donations, the performance indicators for measuring operating efficiency are as shown in Box 7.10. It is also possible to evaluate the operating efficiency in terms of costs per borrower, that is, operating costs per number of clients. The performance indicator used, which is also accurate for use where there are in-kind donations, is the 'Cost per borrower' (7.10.4). This ratio, in contrast with the previously mentioned indicators of operating efficiency, is not calculated in terms of percentages.

The quality of the loan portfolio

Portfolio quality analysis allows for the monitoring of credit risk of the outstanding portfolio of an MFI. The reasons at the base of the portfolio quality analysis are as follows:

- to monitor credit risk in order to avoid unexpected losses;
- to increase possibility of funding from external investors by presenting a minimal amount of risk;
- to allow donors and NGOs to better understand the performance and sustainability in time of their MFI partners.

The indicators are differentiated by:

- portfolio quality ratios, used for monitoring and the evaluation of portfolio credit;
- loan loss ratios, used to estimate the ability to cover eventual credit losses.

The principal indicators of portfolio quality are (Box 7.11): repayment rate indicators; arrears rate; portfolio at risk; delinquent borrowers. The repayment rate indicators, which indicate how much the MFI has received from beneficiaries, can be calculated either by comparing the sums received including interest and capital with:

- how much is owed at up until that moment (7.11.1);
- how much of the totality of the debt remains outstanding (7.11.2).

In the first instance, the value indicates the repayment percentage with respect to the total amount due at that particular moment; the second indicator, combined with the first, illustrates the percentage of funds in use that are in good-standing with respect to the totality of funds outstanding. This indicator can be a signal of the future repayment capacity of the debtor. The portfolio risk indicator offers a measure of the credit risk of the portfolio which compares the total value of loans outstanding with repayments overdue with the total amount of loans disbursed. An alternative measure of credit risk is the number of insolvent debtors with respect to the total number of debtors (7.11.4).

Box 7.11   Portfolio quality indicators

7.11.1   Repayment rate
Amount received (including prepayments and past due amounts)/Amount due (including past due amount)[9]

7.11.2   Arrears rate
Amount in arrears/Portfolio outstanding (including amounts past due)

7.11.3   Portfolio at risk
Outstanding balance of loans with payments past due/Portfolio outstanding (including amounts past due)

7.11.4   Delinquent borrower
Number of delinquent borrowers/Total number of active borrowers

---

Table 7.1 Portfolio at risk (2004)

	Country	Number of clients	PAR > 30 days
K Rep	*Kenya*	55 400	8.20%
Grameen bank	*Bangladesh*	3 700 000	7.98%
Kafo	*Mali*	93 800	6.40%
Mi Banco	*Peru*	113 500	3.40%
Banco sol	*Bolivia*	71 600	3.00%
Asa	*Bangladesh*	2 773 000	1.70%
Tspi	*Phillippines*	93 000	1.20%
Prizma	*Bosnia Herz.*	12 600	1.20%
Besa	*Albania*	5 500	1.00%
Aba	*Egypt*	40 000	0.70%
Compartamos	*Mexico*	310 000	0.60%
Al Amana	*Morocco*	161 000	0.12%

Source: adapted from <http://www.mixmarket.org/>

Box 7.12 Loan loss indicators

7.12.1 Loan loss reserve indicator

Loan loss reserve for the period/Portfolio outstanding for the period

7.12.2 Loan loss indicator

Amount written off in the period/Average portfolio outstanding for the period

---

The second class of quality indicators measures risk in terms of loss from the total credit disbursed and of the reserves set aside in case of loss (Box 7.12).

7.4.2 Performance indicators of profitability area

The required indicators for measuring profitability performance of MFIs are shown in Box 7.13. The indicators 7.13.1 and 7.13.2 respectively provide a measure of profitability of assets and of equity. They are crucial indicators for managers and investors, especially when the MFI is seeking private equity. Adjustments to net operating income after taxes are necessary when the inflation rate and currency risk are relatively high and when in-kind subsidies occur on the balance sheet of the MFI.[10] In-kinds may take the form of paid in capital for financial and non-financial services provided to the MFI.

Box 7.13 Profitability indicators

7.13.1   Adjusted return on assets (AROA)
Adjusted net operating income after taxes/Average total assets

7.13.2   Adjusted return on equity (AROE)
Adjusted net operating income after taxes/Average total equity

7.13.3   Yield on gross portfolio
Cash financial revenue from gross loan portfolio/Average gross loan portfolio

7.13.4   Yield on gross portfolio (real)
(Yield on gross portfolio (nominal) – (Inflation rate)/(1 + Inflation rate)

7.13.5   Adjusted profit margin
Adjusted net operating income/Adjusted operating revenue

The use of average values for the assets and the equity items empha-
sizes the necessity of considering the fluctuation in the two accounting aggregates. In order to focus on the core business of MFIs
(portfolio management), indicators 7.13.3, 7.13.4 and 7.13.5 can be
used. The difference between the former two ratios lies in the fact that
while the first is a measure of earnings by way of returns produced
from the average gross loan portfolio, the second indicator offers the
same measure accounting for the presence of inflation, which is a
noteworthy factor in the context of microfinance. Ratio 7.13.5 is an
average measure of the profitability of each financial product/service
provided.

7.4.3   Performance indicators of sustainability area

The sustainability indicators can be classified in respect of the
taxonomy proposed in Chapter 4 (Box 7.14). The operational self-
sufficiency ratio indicates whether or not enough revenue has been
earned to cover operational costs (these also include inflation costs,
loan loss provisions and currency risk loss provisions). It is important to
verify if the MFI can be defined as sustainable without considering the
support of financial subsidies (grants and soft debts). In this case, ratio
7.14.2, including the cost of debt and the cost of equity, should be considered. Both indicators should calculate the operating revenue
adjusted for the inflation rate.

Box 7.14   Self-sufficiency indicators

7.14.1   Operational self-sufficiency (OSS)

Adjusted Operating revenues/(Operational costs + inflation costs + loan loss provisions + currency risk loss provisions)

7.14.2   Fully financial self-sufficiency (FFSS)

Adjusted Operating revenues/(Operational costs + inflation costs + loan loss provisions + currency risk loss provisions + financial costs)

7.4.4   Performance indicators of leverage and financial structure area

The leverage and financial structure indicators measure the composition of liabilities in order to provide information on the adequacy of the MFI's financial structure (Box 7.15). MFIs have different sources of funds. Equity can be distinguished in invested capital (member shares and investments by outsiders), institutional capital (retained earnings and reserves), debt capital (subordinated debt). MFIs can also borrow funds from institutional and private investors (market loans and client deposits) and may receive grants from private and public donors. Capital is a stable source of funds and it is a buffer against risks but it

---

Box 7.15   Leverage and financial structure indicators

7.15.1   Leverage ratio
Average equity/Average debentures

7.15.2   Equity ratio
Average equity/Total liabilities

7.15.3   Financial debt ratio
Average financial debts/Total liabilities

7.15.4   Soft loan ratio
Average soft loans/Total liabilities

7.15.5   Grant ratio
Average grants/Total liabilities

7.15.6   Subsidy ratio
Average (soft loans + grants)/Total liabilities

---

is costly; debt can be more volatile, but also less costly than equity (in particular, soft loans); grants are the less stable source of funds but they are, by definition, free. Thus, a different composition of funding may impact on the MFI's overall performance and can be taken as a measure of how financially viable it is in the medium and long term. Moreover, the funding structure affects the capability of the MFI by taking advantage of the business opportunities.

7.4.5   Accounting adjustments for performance evaluation

The accounting adjustments for performance measurement can be classified in four categories: subsidy adjustments, inflation adjustments, adjustments for non-performing loans, adjustments for currency gains/losses (Box 7.16). The required accounting adjustments for the analysis of subsidies received must perform the following two tasks:

- to make comparable the performance of MFIs receiving subsidies with those that do not receive subsidies;
- to analyse the degree of dependence of the MFI's economic-financial balance on subsidies.

The adjustments for inflation are performed because the accounting values reported in the financial statements of the MFIs can be significantly affected by the increase in operating expenses when the macroeconomic context in which the institutions operate is characterized by inflation.

Box 7.16   Accounting adjustments

7.16.1   Subsidy adjustments

- subsidized cost of funds adjustment;
- in-kind subsidy adjustments;
- donations.

7.16.2   Inflation adjustments

7.16.3   Adjustments for non-performing loans

- adjustment of loan loss reserves;
- provisional expenditures;
- adjustments for write offs;
- reversal of interest accrued on non-performing loans.

7.16.4   Adjustments for currency gains/losses

The corrections, thus, allow for comparability of the financial statements and the performance indicators in time and in space. The adjustments for non-performing loans are necessary in order to offer relevant economic and financial information to the stakeholders in line with the effective earnings potential of the institution. In fact, the adjustments are justified by the fact that they illustrate the results effectively realized and those that can reasonably be expected according to prudential accounting standards. The adjustments for the currency gains/losses take into account the different currencies in which the values of the operation are expressed. In time, the fluctuation of the exchange rate can produce significant variations in the financial accounting related to the activity on the balance sheet, thus the loans disbursed and the credits recovered, and to the liabilities structure, in particular, related to the financial debts of the institution.

7.5 Conclusion

In the field of microfinance, performance evaluation can be in reference to individual projects as well as to the microfinance institutions overall. Thus, this chapter proposes two performance evaluation models: the first model is for the analysis of a single project, the second model is to evaluate MFIs. The single project approach focuses on six main topics: management, cash flow, earnings, portfolio quality, outreach and subsidies dependence. These topics have been chosen in strict derivation from the main problematic aspects of a project: its equilibrium is a function directly related to the ability of people working on it (*management* analysis), on the possibility of recovering the equilibrium of cash dynamics (*cash flow* analysis), which depends on the ability to monitor the risk–return profile of the project (*earning* and *portfolio quality* analysis) and, finally, on the opportunity to have subsidies both in-kind and money (*subsidies dependence* analysis). Only if these conditions are satisfied will the microfinance project achieve its outreach goals (*outreach* analysis).

The model evaluation proposed for MFIs identifies four different areas: management, profitability, sustainability, leverage and financial structure. From this perspective, a new set of indicators has been suggested. Because of the distinctive features of microfinance, in order to reach goals of sustainability and outreach, the proposed model uses accounting adjustments, necessary to better realize the comparability of performance in space and over time, and utilizes adjustments for subsidy, inflation, non-performing loans, currency gains/losses.

In summary, performance analysis models should be significant tools for the evaluation of microfinance projects and MFIs from a risk management perspective; they allow for an ongoing monitoring of the activities and to the eventual intervention to correct and improve final performance.

8
The Role of Regulation

Gianfranco Vento

8.1 Introduction

Modern microfinance presents some features that imply a revision of regulation and supervision features adopted so far. First of all, it has extensively been pointed out how the range of products and services offered by MFIs has significantly grown throughout the years, including services that are not strictly financial – such as 'social intermediation' services – as well as financial services, which imply a greater management complexity for MFIs and more risks for the overall financial system. Moreover, the number of intermediaries that offer microfinance services has widely increased, and a larger variety of typology of institutions that offer small-amount financial services to financially excluded customers has also developed. Finally, following the Goals of the Millennium, the number of clients that have been reached by microfinance institutions has significantly increased.

Such phenomena – along with the opportunity for microfinance institutions to improve deposit services, also in order to increase their self-sufficiency – have contributed to raising credit, and financial and operating risks that apply to the microfinance field. However, concerning risk typologies, MFIs are significantly different from other regulated financial intermediaries, since regulatory approaches usually applied by supervision authorities do not fully apply to the microfinance sector. Because of the higher variety and wideness of the services, and to the differences among issuing institutions, from a theoretical and practical point of view there is a wide spectrum of different approaches regarding regulation and supervision on MFIs. Such differences vary significantly: according to one approach, microfinance should not be regulated or does not require a specific regulation anyhow; on the other hand, some

think that MFIs need a specific normative body and an appropriate supervision authority.

Since MFIs, in respect of governance structures and of products and services that they provide, significantly differ from country to country, it is not possible to identify an adequate regulation model that can apply for every single regional area in which microfinance institutions operate. Therefore, this chapter focuses on the main variables that should be considered when deciding if MFIs' regulation is suitable and provides some indications on which regulation and supervision instruments should be preferred. In order to do so – by following the essential guidelines of traditional supervision on financial intermediaries – the main determinants of regulation and also the key variables that can significantly influence MFIs' risks are investigated, so that it is possible to draw up a flexible logical scheme of regulation and supervision that can be applied to different operational contexts.

8.2   Regulation, supervision and microfinance

Regulation is defined as the complex of principles and norms that discipline the structure and the operations of financial markets' intermediaries. *Supervision* derives directly from regulation and consists in the punctual verification of the observance of the provisions that have been drawn up within the regulation. The motivation for which a certain industrial sector is regulated derives from the possibility of a market failure. As to the financial system, public authorities use different instruments to promote *stability, efficiency* and *competitiveness* in markets and intermediaries. Along with these principles, which are almost unanimously agreed, most of the authorities that monitor the correct functioning of financial systems focus particularly on the *transparency* of markets and of financial intermediaries and on their correct behaviour, in order to protect the less-informed subjects operating in financial systems. The provisions that regulate operations of financial intermediaries derive from the above points, focusing in particular on the intermediaries' assumption of risks and on the monitoring activities of supervising authorities on the observance of such regulations and of the following principles.

The definition phase of the most suitable scheme of regulation and supervision for MFIs implies certain choices to be made on:

- the goals to be achieved while regulating the sector;
- the different typologies of regulation that are available, concerning *structural* principles that define the morphology of the specific financial

system, *prudential* principles to limit risk assumption for each intermediary, *protective* principles that safeguard the interest of less-informed
customers and principles of *transparency* of operations;
- the available instruments for supervision authorities, based on the
above typologies of regulation;
- the intensity of the required corrective interventions.

The final goals of regulation described above – *stability, efficiency, competitiveness, conduct of business* and *transparency* – present a significant level
of idiosyncrasy; therefore they cannot all be pursued at the same time
and with the same intensity by authorities. Instead, in modern financial
systems, the different forms of regulation listed above tend to be complementary rather than alternative. Such approaches are based on a wide
variety of instruments, of which only some can apply to microfinance.

8.3   Determinants for regulating microfinance

There are many questions to address when regulating microfinance. The
first question concerns whether MFIs should follow the same regulating
criteria used for other typologies of formal financial intermediaries
(banks primarily) or if they need a specific regulating and supervising
system. The answer to this question is significantly influenced by the
adopted definition of microfinance and, consequently, by the border-
line between microfinance and traditional finance. Those who are
inclined towards specific regulation search for the main principles that
may inspire such a set of rules. The questions regarding the suitability of
only applying existing regulation to MFIs and the ones concerning the
extent of regulation and supervision of MFIs have ambiguous solutions
due to the existence of significant trade-offs. Therefore, it is necessary to
analyse the regulation goals mentioned above, which are submitted to
the motivations that promote the regulation of financial systems, in
order to ascertain if the same exigencies also exist in the microfinance
sector.

The goals of regulation

As regards *stability* profiles, one theory claims that MFIs don't need a
specific supervision, since the funded amounts tend to be modest, therefore without implying systemic risks in case one or more MFIs were to
face a situation of bankruptcy (Table 8.1). Moreover, the lack of systemic
risk – and, therefore, the inopportuneness of a specific regulation – is
pointed out in relation to the fact that a significant percentage of MFIs

Table 8.1 The goals of supervision in traditional financing and in microfinance

	Typology of financial intermediaries	
	Traditional intermediaries	Microfinance institutions
Goals of supervision:		
Stability	• Systemic risk monitoring, especially for banks	• Limited monetary function • Low systemic risk
Efficiency	• Monitoring of allocation and operative efficiency in order to protect long-term stability	• Allocation efficiency not lower than traditional financial intermediaries • Improvable operative efficiency
Competitiveness	• Competitiveness monitored in order to enhance long-term stability	• Regulatory restrictions may even reduce competitiveness of some MFIs
Conduct of business and transparency	• Correctness and transparency in customers' relationships • Information transparency for stakeholders	• Correctness and transparency in customers' relationships • Information transparency for stakeholders

only supply microcredit without carrying out a real monetary function and without being closely linked to other financial intermediaries, which could imply risks of contagion.

Concerning the opportunity of regulating microfinance in order to enhance the sector's *efficiency* – especially the allocative efficiency – one of the distinctive features of microfinance is that MFIs, by definition, are predominantly addressed to financially excluded customers who, nonetheless, have a recovery rate equal or higher than that of clients receiving credits from the formal financial system. Therefore, from an operational point view, MFIs show a level of screening and monitoring of their customers that is not lower than the standards of formal financial intermediaries, which are subject to supervision. Such elements do not necessarily suggest that MFIs' regulation is recommended in order to increase their efficiency. On the other hand, some improvements seem to be necessary in order to strengthen the MFIs' operational efficiency; however, such stricter regulation may reduce the strongest features of microfinance institutions so far, which consist in high flexibility and innovation capabilities.

The links between regulation and *competitiveness* also do not seem to unanimously provide elements that suggest a major competitiveness of regulated MFIs rather than non-regulated ones, except the fact that the institutions that undergo a prudential regulation, due to higher management and report tie-ups with the supervising authorities, may result – under the same conditions – having higher burdens compared to non-regulated MFIs.

The most valid arguments suggesting that regulation and, consequently, supervision are necessary for microfinance institutions are based on the aim to achieve – as for traditional intermediaries – an adequate standard in the conduct of businesses and in the *transparency* of MFIs, in order to safeguard the interest of the depositors as well as the less-informed customers in general. Such need derives from a principal–agent problem, where the microfinance institution (the agent) may undertake activities that involve higher risks than those of which the depositors (the principals) are aware, although the negative effects of such activities would fall back on the depositors themselves. The possible excessive risk assumption by MFIs, in a context in which the depositors would not be fully aware of the actual risks of the intermediary, due to asymmetric information, could lead to the insolvency of the MFI, which would consequently affect the depositors rate of return. The relevance of an agent-related problem would have considerably heavier consequences if the customers were very poor subjects with limited capabilities of assessing the risks related to MFIs.

Typologies of supervision

As regards the possible supervision typologies to be adopted, there are different options concerning the use of structural, prudential, transparency and conduct of business controls for MFIs.

Structural supervision operates within the morphology of the sector. Certain structural supervision bodies, which verify the minimum requirements to access the market and limit certain categories of operations, seem necessary also for those scenarios in which microfinance activities are very modest. On the other hand, *prudential controls* act on the efficiency and the sustainability of intermediaries and are based on capital and organizational adequacy criteria, in relation to the assumed risks. These seem to be appropriate in more advanced and complex operative contexts, yet they require higher skills by the supervising authorities. Finally, *transparency* and *conduct of business controls* are intended to guarantee the transparency of the negotiations between the MFI and the clients in order to protect the clients who, typically, are less informed

subjects. Moreover, such controls concern the circulation of accounting and non-accounting information that MFIs must provide to the stakeholders. These do seem necessary in the different sectors of microfinance, although it is difficult to imagine their verification for smaller institutions operating in remote contexts.

The available instruments to supervise MFIs are specifically covered in section 8.5. Hence, it is advisable briefly to concentrate on the *depth* of the due interventions. Alongside considerations on the different interests that should be protected – which depend on the demand of regulation and determine the choice of using or not using regulation and its typologies of approach – there are other peculiar evaluations in microfinance which should direct the supervising authorities in choosing whether to adopt regulation and the instruments that should be used. First of all, it is widely agreed that excessive regulation would suffocate the sector by limiting its development and innovation capabilities. In many developing countries microfinance institutions are still fairly small and they predominantly offer credit products; therefore, an excessively strict prudential regulation would compromise the suitability of many institutions to operate in microfinance, consequently leading to a market failure. Likewise, an excessively strict regulation that determines the operational boundaries of MFIs could limit the institutions' flexibility – commonly considered one of the key features of the microfinance market – and their capacity to identify innovative solutions. The net effect of regulation could be a reduction in microfinance supply, which is the result that those who support regulation want to avoid. Therefore, policy-makers deciding which regulation to implement must consider the overall soundness of the financial system, but also innovation. Indeed, such considerations also apply to more developed countries, in which MFIs are rarely regulated in a specific way, where these institutions end up having the same regulations of traditional financial intermediaries – which are totally inappropriate owing to complexity and structure – or are subject to common law principles that do not identify any supervisory instrument on MFIs.

Other variables

Another aspect regarding MFIs' regulation widely analysed focuses on the comparison between the *costs of regulation and supervision* and the benefits that derive from their adoption. In fact, in many developing countries it is undeniable that public authorities have more urgent interventions that require the low public funds available, rather than performing supervision on microfinance institutions. Moreover, the

lack of adequately trained personnel in the supervision bodies and the absence of an adequate accountancy in MFIs, that should systematically follow principles of truth and fairness, make the supervision activities in developing countries even more difficult. On the other hand, among the reasons that suggest the need to regulate and supervise MFIs, it is often recalled how higher stability of such institutions, by means of specific controls, could improve their capacity to collect private and donors' funds, therefore contributing to the sector's development.

Another variable, regarding the decision of regulating MFIs, that must be considered, concerns the link between the institution and the pursuit of a financial inclusion objective. The ideal regulatory approach should take into consideration the wider objective of contributing to creating a more advanced and inclusive financial system.

Finally, as pointed out in Chapter 5, MFIs are exposed to many of the risks that concern traditional financial intermediaries, yet with different features. For example, the credit-only institutions that operate in a limited geographical area inevitably end up having a low diversification of their loans portfolio; therefore, the prudential requirements of banks – based on concepts of loans portfolio diversification that MFIs do not have – are not in line with the operations of many microfinance institutions. Such consideration also supports an independent regulatory framework for microfinance.

The disquisition regarding the different instruments that should be used in order to protect the various interests of those operating in microfinance – donors, MFIs, beneficiaries, supervision authorities – must also consider some contextual elements that influence the drawing up of the regulations and the actual possibility of applying them. The first consideration regards the types of institutions that have to supervise MFIs. Although the majority of regulations state that the same authorities that supervise banks should also control MFIs (typically, central banks or specialized divisions of the Ministry of Finance), in some cases hybrid solutions are applied, which include non-governmental bodies' activities, self-regulation of groups of MFIs, or the involvement of international rating agencies, which operate under the assignment of the national supervision authorities.

8.4   Key variables for microfinance regulation

In consideration of the elements mentioned above, the analysis of the most suitable regulation and supervision to be implemented for microfinance should be developed considering four main criteria (Table 8.2).

Table 8.2 Key variables for regulation of MFIs

	I Nature of MFIs	II Typology of activity	III Origin of funds	IV Systemic risk
Relevant elements	Distinction among: informal institutions – semiformal institutions – formal institutions	Nature of activity carried out: A. credit-only B. collecting deposits C. other financial services	Distinction among: – donor funds – members' funds – public funds	– Development and age of the industry – Relative intermediated volume
Potential scenarios	– Semiformal institutions (NGOs) are usually credit-only institutions; as far as they collect deposits, they are required to be registered and to assume a different legal and organizational structure – The other MFIs can collect deposits too	A. Institutions that offer credits to their members or to the public B. Institutions that offer credits and collect deposits (time deposits or demand depostits) C. Institutions that offer microinsurance, payments and other financial services	– Institutions that collect donor's funds usually offer microcredits only – MFIs that collect members' funds usually use them to finance other members – MFIs that offer deposits to the public use them for financial intermediation	A. Young expanding microfinance market, in which a low percentage of overall funds are intermediated B. Mature microfinance market, where MFIs intermediate a significant percentage of funds

Continued

Table 8.2 Continued

	I Nature of MFIs	II Typology of activity	III Origin of funds	IV Systemic risk
Suggested approach to regulation	– Credit-only NGOs need a very limited attention form regulators – Credit unions and microfinance banks should be registered and meet less onerous capital requirement and organizational architecture – Downscaling commercial banks should be treated according to the 'Banking Law'	– For A institutions, transparency requirements are suggested but not always compulsory – B institutions should be regulated from a specific agency or by the central bank, according to the nature of MFIs – C institutions should be regulated by a specific authority, by using structural, prudential and transparency approaches	– Public registration and periodic reporting for all MFIs, also for increasing their capability to attract funds – MFIs that collect public funds should be compliant with a set of tailor-made rules concerning market structure and prudential rations (market entry, minimum capital requirements, organization, reporting and deposit insurance)	– Under A scenario, soft regulation based on self-regulation schemes and two-tier entities – Under B scenario, tailored regulation on microfinance concerning entry and structural requirements, prudential ratios, organization, reporting and deposit insurance

Source: Adapted from Vento (2004)

The first aspect to consider is the *nature of the MFIs* somehow to be regulated, by analysing institutions that have different legal structures, governance procedures, target clients and goals (distinguished, for descriptive reasons, in informal, semi-formal and formal institutions), which must be considered according to the various approaches. The second crucial factor which suggests if and how to regulate MFIs is the *typology of activity* carried out by MFIs; particularly, the most sensitive distinction is among credit-only institutions, entities that collect savings and intermediaries that provide other financial services not included in intermediation in a strict sense, such as payments, micro-insurance or micro-venture-capital. The third criterion to take into account is the *origin of funds* used in order to provide microfinance services. Under this profile there are different interests to be preserved in case the MFIs utilize public sums, donor funds or members' savings. The last aspect to analyse is the assessment of *systemic risk* deriving from microfinance. This depends mainly on the development of the industry in the country, on the industry's age and on the volumes intermediated by MFIs in the financial system.

Nature of MFIs

The first criterion addressed here concerns the nature of MFIs, where the distinction usually performed regards informal, semi-formal and formal institutions.[1] Having said that informal institutions are not part of this analysis, since at present there are no forms of regulation and supervision dedicated to such intermediaries, the elements that are considered refer to formal institutions (downscaling commercial banks and the various typologies of microfinance banks) and to semi-formal institutions (mainly financial non-governmental organizations and other mutual credit entities).

The most significant aspects to deepen regarding the nature of MFIs and their regulation are legal structures, the borders of their activities and their internal organization. As mentioned before, as far as semi-formal entities operate as credit-only institutions, they usually receive very limited attention from regulators; in all the cases where these begin to offer savings facilities they are required to assume a different legal status, to be registered, with a well-defined capital in order to be compliant to prudential ratios and to implement internal control functions. These institutions, therefore, should then be regulated coherently with their new nature. Formal institutions, on the other hand, considering their deposit-taking nature, as well as their difficulties in raising capital and their goal of sustainability, have to be regulated by a specific set of

structural and prudential rules, which, however, should prescribe less stringent capital requirements and an easier organizational structure than banks. Last, downgrading commercial banks, which by definition are fully regulated banks according to the national 'Banking Law', do not seem to need particular requirements if compared with other banks, because they continue to perform not only microfinance services; therefore, in most countries they continue to be supervised and regulated as usual banks.

Typology of activity

According to the second criterion, the choices regarding regulation and supervision are based on the nature of the activities that are performed by microfinance entities. All the institutions that provide credits as a unique financial service are characterized by a very low contribution to the overall systemic risk and, by definition, they do not imply problems for the safety of the depositors. Therefore, they are often not regulated, even if some countries require from them transparency standards and the control of unfair practices (the so-called 'conduct of business' reporting). Of course, whenever a MFI does not limit its activity to credit supply, yet collects savings and sometimes offers payment instruments, the institution is almost everywhere forced to be converted to a regulated entity (commonly a bank), or assumes the status of 'microfinance bank' where a specific regulation exists. Such conversion, as obvious, implies the respect of all entry requirements, of minimum capital requirements and prudential ratios, as well as of periodical reporting. Last, for those institutions offering other financial services, it seems opportune to adopt a regulatory approach similar to credit-only institutions, if the only peculiarity is represented by the lending methodology; on the other hand, for those MFIs that intend to provide more complex financial service, such as payments, micro-insurance or micro-venture-capital, a specific regulation is strongly recommended.

Origin of funds

The third relevant criterion in order to determine regulatory policy is the provenance of funds used by MFIs. Whenever this money is donated by third-party organizations, these usually are supposed to have the appropriate instruments in order to assess the MFI they intend to finance; furthermore, in absence of specific regulations, donors can prevent unfair practices by monitoring the selected institutions and requiring them specific reporting on the use of funds. The policy considerations are significantly different when funds are provided by

the public or by members of mutual credit entities or savings banks. In this case, the presence of asymmetric information between depositors and MFIs is often adduced as the main reason for which regulation and supervision are required. In fact, depositors are exposed to moral hazard due to the risk of savings absorption in the event of MFIs' crises. As regards the third criterion, in light of the above, the most suitable approach of the ideal regulation to be adopted must be diversified according to the source of funds. All MFIs, whatever their source of funding, in order to improve their capability to attract money should be required to be registered publicly and produce periodic reporting (including at least credit methodologies, portfolio concentration, credit provisioning and write-offs) to be addressed to a specific regulatory body – where microfinance market is a significant portion of the financial system – or to the authority in charge of supervising the financial system in case of absence of a specific regulatory institution. Those entities that collect public funds should be compliant with a set of tailor-made rules concerning market entry, minimum capital ratios, organization and deposit insurance. These regulations on one hand should impose milder capital requirements than banks and on the other hand they should delimitate the potential activity, and therefore the risk, that these entities could run.

Systemic risk

As far as the last criterion is concerned, when microfinance used to be a marginal phenomenon that involved a few credit-only NGOs and a small number of beneficiaries, there was no need to think about the opportunity to regulate, because regulation and supervision are expensive public goods. Moreover, in some developing countries, it is more likely that these goods are involved in a host of principal–agent failure such as corruption, which often makes unsuccessful any effort to supervise microfinance institutions. Given their nature of expensive public goods, regulation and supervision should be used in the areas with the highest payoffs in terms of systemic risk mitigation.

According to the literature and to the experiences of the past years, in the vast majority of countries microfinance does not create systemic risk, given the small amount of loans and the very limited access to the payment system of MFIs, where it exists. Therefore, in all the countries where the systemic relevance of microfinance is limited, a vast number of authors agree on a soft regulation, essentially based on public registration (licensing), or suggest the implementation of self-regulation

schemes and second-tier regulation (delegated regulation), performed by other actors such as rating agencies.

Also the development of the industry in the country and the volumes intermediated by MFIs in the financial system affect the decision about how to regulate and the instruments to adopt. Particularly, the need to design a specific regulatory framework for microfinance institutions is especially felt in the countries where those institutions are significant actors in the financial market; otherwise, the most common solution that is adopted is to regulate under Banking Law those entities that collect deposits and offer loans, whereas credit-only organizations are often in a shadow area, without any explicit regulation or supervision.

The combination of all the above criteria creates a peculiar picture that varies according to the country, and therefore it is not possible to imagine a single regulatory approach suitable for microfinance industries world-wide.

8.5   Which instruments to adopt

In order to achieve the above-mentioned goals of stability, efficiency, competitiveness and transparency, the instruments available for the authorities that regulate and supervise microfinance institutions are sometimes drastically different compared with the traditional instruments and procedures adopted for traditional financial intermediaries. Such instruments can be split in two macro categories that refer to *structural, protective* and *transparency* supervision instruments, as well as to *prudential* supervision.

The main variables that can be used to organize a framework that follows the said goals in the microfinance market include:

- structural supervision: rules to access the market and operational restrictions for MFIs;
- protective supervision: insurance schemes for depositors;
- transparency supervision: compulsory transparency on the conditions applied to clients and compulsory information for stakeholders.

As regards *prudential supervision*, the regulating instruments that can be used for the microfinance sector are essentially based on minimum capital requirements, capital adequacy coefficients, compulsory scheduled reporting, minimum liquidity ratios and on certain rules on governance and organizational structures of the institutions under supervision, as for traditional financial intermediaries.

At present, these instruments are used only in some countries in which MFIs operate and they are highly diversified depending on the operational contexts. The different regulation and supervision approaches significantly depend on the specific features of the institutions that regulate and supervise MFIs, which include solutions that can range from a supervision performed by the same authority that supervises traditional financial intermediaries – typically, the central bank – to self-regulation schemes, which consist in rules of conduct agreed by a group of collaborating MFIs and, sometimes, define a centralized internal structure in charge of monitoring the compliance with such principles. An example of specific regulatory rules for MFIs is represented by the Peruvian case (Box 8.1). Therefore, a possible analysis could focus on how different regulation and supervision instruments can be combined with the criteria that determine the choice of regulating microfinance, as described in the previous section. Table 8.3 describes the results of such analysis.

If the MFIs operating in the market are basically NGOs – which offer low-amount credit products and manage lower volumes than the banking system without collecting public savings – the inappropriateness of applying strict regulation is widely agreed. In such cases, in fact, systemic risk is low and the costs of supervision would not be compensated by the possible benefits that such supervision would provide. Since NGOs don't have a minimum capital required, prudential supervision is inappropriate in such contexts. In this case, regulation must be minimized, provided that MFIs must be registered with the supervision authority of the financial system and that a scheduled report of the granted micro-credits is compulsory, in order to monitor the overall performance of the microfinance sector and, therefore, to prevent potential problems that may jeopardize the stability of the financial system.

As MFIs offer a wider range of products and services, collect public deposits and operate with significant volumes of financial resources, authorities need to increase their attention. This implies a specific regulation that provides the organizational minimum requirements in order to access the market. Moreover, control units inside the MFIs must be created in order to control risks, the minimum capital requirements and the capital adequacy coefficients. Regarding the capital, the majority of existing regulations agree to have lower requirements for MFIs than for banks, yet to have higher solvency coefficients, in order to partially compensate for the low diversification of the loans portfolio.

In addition, the rules of microfinance, in order to encourage the development of the sector and fight financial exclusion, should consider

Box 8.1 Regulated MFIs: a taxonomy of Peruvian institutions

In Peru formal MFIs are regulated by a public agency, the 'Superintendencia de Banca y Seguros' (SBS). Microfinance institutions and the activities they perform undergo the same regulations that are applied to banks and other Peruvian financial intermediaries, except some differences in the minimum capital requirements and in the range of permitted operations.

Peruvian MFIs that are subject to regulation are divided as follows:

1. Municipal Saving and Loan Institutions (MSLI), also known as CMAC (Caja Municipal de Ahorro y Credito);
2. Rural Saving and Loan Institutions (RSLI), also known as CRAC (Caja Rural de Ahorro y Credito);
3. Entities for Development of the Small and Microenterprise (EDPYME).

The financial services that the microfinance institutions can offer vary according to the nature of the different MFIs. CMACs began their activities around 1980 and were created in collaboration with the German government; they are owned by local authorities and operate in the provinces by supporting economic activities carried out by low-income subjects. They are allowed to offer deposits, pension schemes, current accounts, personal and small corporate loans and also to carry out operations abroad. They cannot collect savings and provide collateral loans during their first year of activities and they cannot provide microfirms with loans for the first three years.

On the other hand, CRACs were created in the early 1990s, after the Banco Agrario was closed because of financial reform. These are owned by local private firms and mainly operate in rural areas. They cannot offer savings passbooks, time deposits and current accounts.

EDPYME were created in the mid 1990s in order to formalize the NGOs that were offering loans to microfirms. Such formalization became increasingly important after the approval, at the end of the decade, of a law that required NGOs pay a tax on the interests gained from the loans they granted. Because NGOs had little experience in collecting public funds, EDPYMEs became credit-only institutions. In particular, EDPYMEs can only offer credit and can obtain the necessary resources from banks, from the capital market, and can also be financed by COFIDE (a second-tier bank established in 1992 to finance medium- and long-term private activities and micro and small enterprises). With the authorization of SBS and with a minimum capital of 1.4 million USD, EDPYME can also collect public deposits.

Microfinance banks, instead, can offer all financial services. The minimum capital to establish a microfinance bank is US$5.3 million. Vice versa, for EDPYMEs, CMACs and CRACs the minimum capital is US$241 000. All MFIs have to be authorized by SBS to open their branches. At the end of 2004 there were 40 MFIs, with total assets of US$1.2 billion, representing 5.8 per cent of the total assets of the entire financial system.

Table 8.3 Key variables and instruments for regulating MFIs

Nature of MFIs	Semi-formal	Formal		
Typology of MFIs	NGOs	Credit unions	Microfinance banks	Commercial banks
Typology of activities	• microcredits	• microcredits • deposits	• microcredits • deposits • other services	• microcredits • deposits • other services
Source of funds	• donors	• members	• public	• public
Systemic risk	• low	• low	• medium	• high
Principles of structural supervision	• operational restrictions	• market access rules • operational restrictions	• market access rules • operational restrictions	• market access rules • operational restrictions
Principles of protective supervision	• compulsory registration to reduce the risk of frauds	• depositors' insurance, also by means of deposits in supervised banks	• insurance of deposits as in the banking system	• insurance of deposits as in the banking system
Principles of transparency	• transparency rules on applied conditions and on processes	• transparency rules on applied conditions • minimum compulsory disclosure of accountancy information	• transparency rules on applied conditions • minimum compulsory disclosure of accountancy information	• transparency rules on applied conditions • minimum compulsory disclosure of accountancy information

Continued

Table 8.3 Continued

Nature of MFIs	Semi-formal	Formal		
Typology of MFIs	NGOs	Credit unions	Microfinance banks	Commercial banks
Principles of prudential supervision		• minimum capital requirements • minimum liquidity • organizational and governance requirements	• minimum capital requirements • capital adequacy coefficients • minimum liquidity coefficients • organizational and governance requirements	• minimum capital requirements • capital adequacy coefficients • minimum liquidity coefficients • organizational and governance requirements
Supervisors	• executive power • supervision authority on banks • self-regulating institutions • rating agencies	• supervision authority on banks • self-regulating institutions • rating agencies	• supervision authority on banks	• supervision authority on banks

three other aspects, regardless of which institutions provide the services: depositors' insurance, the offer of credit information services and the interest rate caps. As for the first, those who deposit their savings in a regulated microfinance institution must receive the same guarantees that the depositors of formal intermediaries receive on the reimbursement of their deposits, or of part of them, in case the MFI struggles to repay.

The offer of credit information databases, which collect information on marginal and unregistered clients, is an objective that MFIs will necessarily have to aim for, in order to reduce the information unbalances which physiologically belong to microfinance. Such systematic collection of information can also be performed by local associations of MFIs, yet it definitely has to be supported in its initial stages by an institutional intervention, in order to define the criteria of the collection and the use of such data.

Finally, in order to support microfinance, there is the need to take into account the interest rate caps, where they exist. In this matter it is important to point out how, in order to guarantee the sustainability through time and to avoid distortions in the financial market, MFIs usually supply credit services at higher interest rates than market rates. Hence, this element has to be adequately considered when conceiving a regulation for microfinance, with a possible exemption of microfinance institutions from these caps if they appear to be too strict, or requiring MFIs to disclose the method of calculation of the interest rates they fix. The combination of supervision instruments also has to take into account the lack of economic and human resources that can be used for such activities in many developing countries, which are stricken by poverty and weakness in the public control systems and in the judicial system. Moreover, it is necessary to remember that even the best conceived regulation and the more sophisticated supervision approaches turn out to be ineffective in contexts where the supervised institutions present significant deficiencies in the performance of internal control systems and have a governance that neglects the principles of sustainability.

8.6 Conclusion

The growth of the microfinance sector allows the expansion of the offer of financial services to customers that, so far, were not bankable, therefore reducing the rate of financial exclusion. Such a trend, however, could not be considered satisfactory if such an expansion process beyond the traditional borders should cause a higher fragility in the financial system itself and higher risks for those who deposit their savings in MFIs. In the light

of above, there is the need to regulate those institutions that offer more complex services and that operate with third-party funds. With the intent of avoiding the perversion of MFIs and limiting their flexibility and capability in finding innovative solutions in risk management, in distribution techniques and in many more aspects, regulation has to be designed for microfinance institutions, avoiding certain aspects of traditional regulation. Despite the existing structural and operational differences between MFIs around the world, it is possible to identify some common approaches that should suggest how to regulate and supervise MFIs.

In the same way it is possible to identify a number of instruments, provided by the supervision of banks, which, by resorting to some simple tricks, can be used by MFIs. In particular, structural supervision instruments become important – so that authorities are constantly aware of the size and the trends of the market – as well as protective and transparency supervision rules, for the safety of less informed clients, and the principles of prudential supervision, which allow MFIs to maintain the typical operational flexibility with an increased awareness of the assumed risks.

9
The Road Ahead: A Platform for Microfinance

Mario La Torre

9.1 Introduction

Microfinance has changed dramatically over the last few decades. These changes have affected beneficiaries, products and practitioners. The shift from microcredit, intended for the 'poorest of the poor', to microfinance, allocated to all victims of financial exclusion, has created a different microfinance pattern. New customers have introduced new needs, and new needs have brought about new financial products offered not only by NGOs, or non-profit institutions, but also by banks and other financial intermediaries. This new scenario highlights different issues which come together within modern microfinance. These concern the setting for microfinance, policy and strategies for microfinance programmes and institutions, microfinance management objectives and tools, and, finally, microfinance financial structures. These four aspects represent the key variables for modelling a microfinance platform in which markets, authorities, institutions, intermediaries, practitioners and customers could work together to better achieve the final goal.

9.2 The features of modern microfinance

In the light of the changing trend, modern microfinance will be characterized by different features.

Modern microfinance must be transverse (crosswise oriented)

Microfinance is not only microcredit but consists of different financial and technical services offered to respond to the needs of beneficiaries, and to manage the financial and operational risks involved in each transaction. Working towards transverse microfinance means, first of

all, working towards a legal, fiscal and regulatory framework that makes it possible. The recourse to new financial products must be easy, cheap and transparent. Furthermore, operational boundaries of MFIs must be regulated ensuring flexibility, efficiency and stability of each intermediary and of the market as a whole. Financial innovation, both at a product and at a process level, must be feasible and sustainable at the same time. *Modern microfinance needs a new regulatory environment, both in developing countries and in industrialized ones.*

Modern microfinance must be programmatic

This means that every single programme sponsored by international donors, public or private, as well as the composition criteria behind each single MFI portfolio, must be inspired by a planned strategy implemented at an international, national and local level. As such, the role of governmental local bodies is particularly relevant, as they know the territory and the social customs. Thus, they are best able to establish the effective opportunity cost of each single initiative. *Modern microfinance needs to be programmatic in nature in order to maximize the efficacy of projects carried out in specific areas.*

Modern microfinance must be ethical

In Chapter 1, we outlined the main features for an ethically compliant microfinance. As explained, ethicality is not an exclusive goal of the non-profit sectors. Ethical behaviour, the depth of ethicality and the level of intermediation costs require a strong collaboration between the non-profit and profit sectors. To increase the depth of ethicality in terms of extension, transversality and consolidation, the non-profit and profit sectors must work together to implement a transparent operational process, consistent across shareholdings and strategies. To reduce the intermediation cost, the non-profit and profit sectors, together with local governmental bodies, must implement risk management models to ensure a higher degree of efficiency and more accurate pricing policies in order to achieve positive performances that respect the goal of ethicality.

Modern microfinance must be sustainable

Sustainability has been the main goal of modern microfinance over the last decade. Nevertheless, there is still a long way to go. In Chapter 4, we have seen that sustainability in microfinance is a complicated task for at least two reasons. First, the definition of sustainability in microfinance differs from the traditional one. Moreover, microfinance programmes

and institutions may adopt different levels of sustainability. Secondly, sustainability must be reached without compromising outreach. The shift from operational sustainability to financial self-sustainability has been determined mainly by the growing percentage of private investors financing microfinance and by the need for public donors to be more selective in the initiatives they support: financial self-sustainability means good performance; operational sustainability means more attention to outreach. Modern microfinance needs to strike a balance between these two goals. This calls for a big effort from both the non-profit sector and private investors. The non-profit sector must operate primarily to reduce operational costs, in order to achieve greater efficiency. Private investors must collaborate to measure and manage microfinance risks more accurately and to reduce financial costs, while being aware that a higher level of outreach calls for a rate of return lower than the market rate. Higher levels of efficiency, sophisticated risk management and positive rates of return lower than the market rate, facilitate self-sustainable outreach. A combination of efficiency and ethicality is the recipe for a balance between sustainability and outreach. Obviously, this recipe needs a great number of chefs to prepare and serve. Semi-formal and formal MFIs, banks and other financial intermediaries, local and national governmental bodies, together with public donors, are all invited to take up this challenge.

Modern microfinance must be integrated (networked)

The feature of transversality and the need for programmatic, sustainable and ethical initiatives are the variables that characterize modern microfinance and which call for new actors to come into the microfinance market. The offering of new products and services, the need for conscious strategies, the growing attention to sustainability and the difficult task of combining sustainability with ethical goals and outreach requires the effort of different players, each with his own role to play. Microfinance networks must be established considering the non-profit sector (donors, informal and semi-formal MFIs), the traditional financial sector (formal MFIs and other financial intermediaries) and governmental bodies (at an international, national and local level). Each one of these parties can contribute to the achievement of the key features of modern microfinance.

9.3   The microfinance platform: actors and functions

The microfinance network must be implemented considering the different attitudes of the different players, each one of which can play a role in shaping the different features of modern microfinance (Figure 9.1).

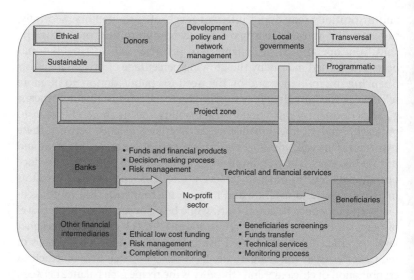

Figure 9.1   Microfinance platform

The role of national/international donors and local governments

Within the microfinance platform, national/international donors, and municipalities and local governmental bodies, have a fundamental role that can be broken down into three main functions. First, as already explained, they can work towards achieving programmatic microfinance by planning microfinance initiatives that meet world-wide and local needs and by selecting those feasible initiatives that present the lowest opportunity costs for the community. Secondly, they can offer technical services, within the programmes sponsored, directly or in collaboration with informal and semiformal institutions.

Donors also offer funds and financial services. In the case of municipalities, this function should be restricted to the coverage of operative expenses or to non-monetary financial services, such as guarantee funds. Through the offer of technical and financial products, donors and local bodies contribute to lowering the intermediation cost of the programme, while avoiding direct involvement in the credit process by financing microcredit funds. This function furthers both the ethicality and sustainability of the initiatives. Finally, donors and municipalities can play the role of network-manager, creating, organizing, managing and monitoring the microfinance network for each single initiative.

As such, donors and local governmental bodies are in the position, once a microfinance project has been selected, to involve different actors of the non-profit and profit sectors in order to implement the most effective operational and financial structure.

The role of banks

Banks and other financial intermediaries are gaining more space in modern microfinance programmes. We saw in Chapter 1 that a greater involvement of profit-oriented institutions in the microfinance market may have positive effects, in terms of efficiency and sustainability, and negative effects, in terms of ethicality and outreach. Thus, the role of banks and financial intermediaries in modern microfinance must tie in with the aim of maximizing the positive effects, while minimizing the negative ones. The network must operate to increase sustainability and outreach at the same time.

In this scenario banks can play different roles in a microfinance network. First, they can ensure private funds to microfinance programmes, sponsoring single projects, investing in share capital of MFIs or creating microfinance special purpose vehicles within the banking group. Secondly, they can carry out the credit decision-making process, and in particular the evaluation of the beneficiaries' creditworthiness. Their expertise in this field would help to achieve a higher economy of scale, especially for those programmes that aim to benefit a large number of customers. Thirdly, banks can contribute to implement risk management models specifically tailored to microfinance projects, increasing the efficiency of the initiatives. Finally, the presence of a bank in microfinance projects facilitates the provisioning of other financial services, in addition to microcredit, such as microleasing, deposits, payments services, thus improving the efficacy and the outreach of the initiatives. Through banks, financial innovation can be made available to microfinance. Microcredit portfolio securitization can be taken as an example of financial innovation enhancing the degree of liquidity stored in the balance sheet of MFIs and facilitating the credit risk management of microcredit portfolios.

Banks' financial and technical services have a cost. Such costs must be covered by revenues, in order to implement a sustainable project, but they should also match the degree of ethicality and the outreach of each single initiative. As a result, banks have two options: financing only those initiatives that ensure a market rate of return or forgoing market return when considering their involvement in microfinance. The first option will restrict the number of microfinance projects to support, in

particular those programmes which penalize outreach over sustainability. The second option will impact negatively on the bank balance sheet because of a lower profit. Nevertheless, bank managers must consider at least two factors: first, that there are ways to reduce the negative impact on profit; secondly, that the value of a bank is also influenced by qualitative aspects, such as ethical behaviour and transparency, which markets and customers are beginning to take into consideration.

With regard to the first point, banks may encourage new ethical practices in order to distribute the opportunity cost implicit in microfinance projects. Some banks, for example, have lowered the intermediation cost asking their employers to devote a certain amount of working hours for free to the microfinance initiatives promoted. Others have devoted stock options revenues to microfinance programmes. Still other banks set aside a certain percentage of customer credit card payments (ethical credit cards) for microfinance initiatives.

With regard to the second point outlined, it is worth remembering that corporate social responsibility is becoming a key variable in banking strategies and microfinance can represent a valid alternative to improve banks' reputations and, through this, banking value.

The role of other financial intermediaries

The goal of lowering the intermediation costs and the need to manage the risks associated with microfinance programmes can be best achieved through the entry of non-bank financial intermediaries in the microfinance market. Therefore, Ethical Investment Funds, Pension Funds and Insurance Companies can play a major role. EIFs and EPFs represent an important source of low-cost funding for microfinance, which remains, as yet, unexploited. Savings collected from ethical investors could find market investment alternatives in microfinance that meet the ethical features required. Moreover, ethical savings do not incorporate a risk–return paradigm similar to traditional savings and, therefore, can be devoted to investments that ensure rate of returns lower than the market. Microfinance networks, then, should operate in order to enforce the role of EIFs and EPFs in microfinance projects.

The role of insurance companies is more related to the managing of financial and non-financial risks and to monitoring. Microfinance needs insurance products specifically tailored for microfinance programmes. This is true not only for financial risk, such as credit risk and market risks, but also for business and process risks. As seen in Chapter 5, the transfer of non-financial risk to third counter-parties is often the only alternative to managing them. Chapter 6 outlined the need for monitoring procedures,

in particular for business and process risks. Nevertheless, insurance products and services raise the cost of microfinance projects. For this reason, the role of local governmental bodies and other public institutions offering guarantee funds, particularly structured with regard to business and process risks, can help in lowering these kinds of costs.

The role of the non-profit sector

The non-profit sector will still play a fundamental role in microfinance. Informal and semi-formal institutions have the important task of preserving the original features of microfinance, notably the ethicality of the business, the flexibility of the organizations/process, and the proximity to the beneficiaries. They must interact with donors and local governments in order to propose projects that tie in with national and local development policies. They are in the position of selecting those beneficiaries who may be more appropriate for the programme. They have the human resources to offer technical assistance to the selected beneficiaries from the first step of the project right up to the exit strategy. They must collaborate with financial intermediaries to implement an efficient credit process that minimizes agency costs, arising from different incentives and asymmetric information, and risk management models that do not jeopardize the flexibility of the procedures. During the project they are in the best position to channel the funds and to act as delegate monitors for public and private investors in order to reach the exit strategy goal.

9.4   Conclusion

Modern microfinance needs a market policy to be successful. This policy can take the form of a microfinance platform which establishes goals, actors and functions and which lays the fundamentals for local, national and international microfinance networks, interacting with each other. The platform must reflect the features of modern microfinance, which aims to be *transversal*, *programmatic*, *ethical* and *sustainable*. These features can be achieved only with the collaboration of different actors, each playing his own role within the network: the non-profit and profit sectors must work together. Local, national and international governmental institutions can act as network managers, devising the platform, promoting the network and monitoring that it is working efficiently, transparently and in compliance with antitrust laws.

Notes

1 A New Conception of Microfinance

1. For further details see Calderon (2002), pp. 73 onwards.
2. For more information on the role of commercial banks in microfinance see Baydas et al. (1997).

2 Products and Services in Modern Microfinance

1. For detail on the categories of beneficiaries and the characteristics of the range of products and services of modern microfinance, see sections 1.3 and 1.4 of Chapter 1.
2. For greater detail on the screening of beneficiaries, see chapter 3, section 3.2.
3. For greater detail, see chapter 3, section 3.5.
4. The Bulgarian Ministry of Employment and Welfare and the United Nations Development Programme (UNDP) have launched a successful project of microleasing. For more information, see: <www.jobs-bg.org>.
5. In India NABARD began to offer credit cards (Kisan Credit Cards – KCC) in 1999. At the end of 2003 the total number of KCC issued was 31.6 million. For more information, see: <www.microsave.it>.
6. For more details see Chapter 5.
7. See section 2.3.
8. For more detail see: <www.mixmarket.org>.

3 The Main Features of Microcredit

1. For further details on microcredit process see also Chapter 6.
2. To deepen the criteria of loan portfolio diversification see Chapter 5.
3. CAMEL is a standardized checklist adopted by banks in order to assess credit risk of the borrowers (see Chapter 7 for details).
4. See Chapters 1 and 5.
5. On sustainability and interest rate policy see Chapter 4.

4 Sustainability and Outreach: the Goals of Microfinance

1. The analytical notation is simplified and adapted from Armendariz de Aghion and Morduch (2005).
2. For deepening the above-mentioned trade-off between sustainability and outreach see, among others, Zeller and Meyer (2002).
3. See Chapter 5.
4. See Chapter 6.
5. See Chapter 9.

5 Risk Management in Microfinance

1. This aspect will be analysed in more detail in Chapter 6.

7 Microfinance Performance

1. Foster, G., 'Financial statement analysis', Prentice Hall, NY, 1986.
2. Different outreach goals include but are not limited to: financing only poor women; financing the 'poorest of the poor'; and financing the urban and/or rural poor. For more details see Chapter 4.
3. Ledgerwood, J., *Microfinance Handbook: An Institutional and Financial Perspective*, International Bank for Reconstruction and Development, Washington, 1998, p. 212.
4. 'Past due amounts' should be defined as those amounts in arrears not paid at the time of calculation of the ratio.
5. For more details see Chapter 4.
6. Westley, G.D., 'Guidelines for monitoring and evaluating projects of the social entrepreneurship program', Washington D.C., 2002. Available at <www.iadb.org/sds/doc/guidelinesmonitoring.pdf>.
7. For the terminology and methodology of calculation of performance indicator see Von Stauffenberg, D., 'Definitions of Selected Financial terms, Ratios and Adjustments for Microfinance', *Microbanking Bulletin*, November 2002.
8. The following indicators can be computed substituting the number of loans and of the active borrowers with the number of deposits and of active depositors.
9. 'Prepayments' should be defined as payments of interest made in advance by beneficiaries for the reimbursement of the funds used. The practice to pay in advance only the interest component and not also the capital component of the amount received is particularly indicated to beneficiaries who need longer time to give back money received.
10. For more details, see section 7.4.5.

8 The Role of Regulation

1. For an overview on the different categories of MFIs see Chapter 1.

Bibliography

Adams, D.W. and D. Fitchett (eds), *Informal Finance in Low-Income Countries* (Boulder: Westview Press, 1992).

Adams, D.W. and R.C. Vogel, 'Rural Financial Markets in Low Income Countries: Recent Controversies and Lessons', *World Development*, 14 (4) (1986).

Adams, D.W, D.H. Graham and J.D. Von Pischke, *Undermining Rural Development with Cheap Credit* (Boulder: Westview Press, 1984).

Adams, D.W., G. Donald and J.D. Von Pischke (eds), *Rural Financial Markets in Developing Countries: Their Use and Abuse* (Baltimore, Md.: Johns Hopkins University Press, 1983).

Adams, D.W. and G.I. Nehman, 'Borrowing Costs and the Demand for Rural Credit', *Journal of Development Studies*, 15 (2) (1979).

Adams, D.W., 'The Case for Voluntary Savings Mobilization: Why Capital Markets Flounder', *Small Farmer Credit: Analytical Papers*, AID Spring Review of Small Farmer Credit, XIX, Washington D.C. (1973).

Aleem, I., 'The Rural Credit Market in Pakistan: The Costs of Screening', in K. Hoff, A. Braverman and J.E. Stiglitz, *The Economics of Rural Organization: Theory, Practice and Policy* (New York: Oxford University Press, 1993).

AMAP, *Measuring Outreach*, Conceptual Workshop Proceedings (2004).

Armendariz de Aghion, B., 'Development Banking', *Journal of Development Economics*, 58 (2) (1999) 83–100.

Armendariz de Aghion, B. and J. Morduch, *The Economics of Microfinance* (Cambridge: MIT Press, 2005).

Associazione Bancaria Italiana, *La Rsi e il Bilancio Sociale nelle Banche e nelle altre imprese* (Rome: Bancaria Editrice, 2003).

Associazione Bancaria Italiana, *Sistemi di controllo interno ed evoluzione dell'Internal Auditing* (Rome, 1999).

Baravelli, M., *Strategia e organizzazione della banca* (Milan: Egea, 2003).

Baravelli, M. and A. Viganò (eds), *L'internal Audit nelle banche* (Rome: Bancaria Editrice, 1999).

Basel Committee on Banking Supervision, *The New Basel Capital Accord, Consultative Paper*, Bank for International Settlements, January, Basel (2001a).

Basel Committee on Banking Supervision, *The New Basel Capital Accord, An Explanatory Note*, Bank for International Settlements, January, Basel (2001b).

Basel Committee on Banking Supervision, *The New Basel Capital Accord*, Basel (2003).

Basel Committee on Banking Supervision, *International Convergence of Capital Measurement and Capital Standards: a Revised Framework*, Bank for International Settlements, June, Basel (2004a).

Basel Committee on Banking Supervision, *Principles for the Management and Supervision of Interest Rate Risk*, Bank for International Settlements, July, Basel (2004b).

Baydas, M.M., D.H. Graham and L. Valenzuela, *Commercial Banks in Microfinance: New Actors in the Microfinance World*, USAID, mimeo (1997).

Bekerman, M., *Microcreditos* (Buenos Aires: Grupo Editorial Norma, 2004).

Bennet, L. and C.E. Cuevas 'Sustainable Banking with the Poor', *Journal of International Development*, 8 (2) (1996) 145–52.

Bennet, L., M. Goldberg and P. Hunte, 'Owneship and Sustainability: Lessons on Group-based Financial Services from South Asia', *Journal of International Development*, 8 (2) (1996) 271–88.

Bennet, L., P. Hunte and M. Goldberg, *Group-Based Financial Systems: Exploring the Links between Performance and Participation* (Washington D.C.: World Bank, 1997).

Besley, T., S. Coate and G. Loury, 'The Economics of Rotating Savings and Credit Associations', *American Economic Review*, 83 (4) (1993).

Bester, H., 'Screening vs. Rationing in Credit Markets with Imperfect Information', *American Economic Review*, 74 (4) (1985).

Bose, P., 'Formal–Informal Sector Interaction in Rural Credit Markets', *Journal of Development Economics*, 56 (1998) 256–80.

Bouman, F.J.A., *Small Short and Unsecured: Informal Finance in Rural India* (Delhi: Oxford University Press, 1989).

Bouman, F.J.A. and O. Hospes (eds), *Financial Landscapes Reconstructed: The Fine Art of Mapping Development* (Boulder: Westview Press, 1994).

Brand, M., *The MBP Guide to new Product Development, ACCION International* (2001).

Braverman, A. and J.L. Guasch, 'Rural Credit Markets and Institutions in Developing Countries: Lessons for Policy Analysis from Practice and Modern Theory', *World Development*, 14 (10/11) (1986).

Brown, W., 'Microinsurance: the Risk, Perils and Opportunities', in M. Harper (ed.), *Microfinance. Evolution, Achievements and Challenges* (London: ITDG Publishing, 2003).

Burkett, P., 'Group Lending Programs and Rural Finance in Developing Countries', *Savings and Development* (1991).

Calderon, M.L., *Microcréditos. De pobres a microempresarios* (Barcelona, Editorial Ariel, 2002).

Carbo, S., E.P.M. Gardner and P. Molyneux, *Financial Exclusion* (London: Macmillan, 2005).

Chorafas, D.N., *Implementing and Auditing the Internal Control System* (New York: Palgrave, 2001).

Chowdhury, O.H., 'Credit in Rural Bangladesh', *Asian Economic Review*, 34 (2) (1992).

Christen, R., 'What Microenterprise Credit Programs Can Learn from the Moneylenders', *Acciòn International Discussion Paper*, No. 4 (1989).

Christen, R., 'Formal Credit for Informal Borrowers: Lessons from Informal Lenders', in D.W. Adams and D. Fitchett (eds), *Informal Finance in Low-Income Countries* (Boulder: Westview Press, 1992).

Christen, R.P., *Banking Services for the Poor: Managing for Financial Success* (Somerville: Acciòn International, 1997).

Christen, R.P., 'Keys to Financial Sustainability', in M.S. Kimenyi, R.C. Wieland and J.D. Von Pischke, *Strategic Issues in Microfinance* (Aldershot: Ashgate, 1998).

Christen, R., E. Rhyne and R. Vogel, 'Maximizing the Outreach of Microenterprise Finance: The Emerging Lessons of Successful Programs', *USAID Program and Operations Assessment Report*, No. 10, Washington D.C. (1995).

Christen, R.P. and R. Rosenberg, 'Regulating microfinance: the options', *Small Enterprise Development*, 11 (4) December (2000).

Coetzee, G., *Regulation and Supervision of Microfinance Institutions: The Experience in South Africa*, mimeo, March (1998).

Conning, J., 'Outreach, Sustainability and Leverage in Monitored and Peer-Monitored Lending', *Journal of Development Economics*, 60 (1999) 51–77.

Consultative Group to Assist the Poorest, 'Format for Appraisal for Microfinance Institutions', *Technical Tool Series*, No. 4, July (1999).

Consultive Group to Assist the Poorest, 'The Rush to Regulate', *Occasional Paper*, No. 4, April (2000).

Consultive Group to Assist the Poorest, 'Guiding Principles on Regulation and Supervision of Microfinance', September (2002).

Consultative Group to Assist the Poorest, 'Microcredit Interest Rate', *Occasional Paper* No. 1, November (2002).

Consultative Group to Assist the Poorest, 'Financial Institution With A Double Bottom Line: Implications For The Future Of Microfinance', *Occasional Paper*, No. 8, July (2004).

Counts, A. and S. Sobhan, *Recommendations for the Creation of a Pro-Microcredit Regulatory Framework*, mimeo, January (2001).

Cracknell, D. and H. Sempangi, 'Product Costing in Practice. The Experience of MicroSave-Africa', *Small Enterprise Development Journal*, 14 (13) (2003).

Devereux, J. and R.P.H. Fishe, 'An Economic Analysis of Group Lending Programs in Developing Countries', *Developing Economies*, 31 (1) (1993).

Diamond, D.W., 'Financial Intermediation and Delegated Monitoring', *Review of Economic Studies*, 51 (1984) 393–414.

Diamond, D.W. and P.H. Dybvig, 'Bank Runs, Deposit Insurance, and Liquidity', *Journal of Political Economy*, 91 (3) (1983).

Donald, G., *Credit for Small Farmers in Developing Countries* (Boulder: Westview Press, 1976).

Drake, D. and E. Rhyne (eds), *The Commercialization of Microfinance: Balancing Business and Development* (Bloomfield: Kumarian Press, 2002).

Egger, P., 'Banking for the Rural Poor: Lessons from some Innovative Savings and Credit Schemes', *International Labour Review*, 125 (1986).

Floro, S.L. and P.A. Yotopoulos, *Informal Credit Markets and the New Institutional Economics: The Case of Philippine Agriculture* (Boulder: Westview Press, 1991).

Forestieri, G., *Corporate and Investment Banking* (Milan: Egea, 2005).

Foster, S., S. Greene and J. Pytkowska, *The State of Microfinance in Central and Eastern Europe and the New Independent States*, Microfinance Centre for Central and Eastern Europe and the New Independent States (2003).

Gallardo, J., *A Framework for Regulating Microfinance Institutions: The Experience in Ghana and Philippines*, World Bank, Financial Sector Development Department, mimeo, November (2001).

Germidis, D., D. Kessler and R. Meghir, *Financial Systems and Development: What Role for the Formal and Informal Financial Sectors?* (Paris: Development Center for the Organization for Economic Cooperation and Development, 1991).

Getubig, I. (ed.), *Overcoming Poverty Through Credit: The Asian Experience in Replicating the Grameen Bank Approach* (Kuala Lumpur: APDC, 1993).

Getubig, I., J. Remenyi and B. Quinones (eds), *Creating the Vision: Microfinancing the Poor in Asia-Pacific: Issues Constraints and Capacity Building* (Kuala Lumpur: Asia Pacific Development Centre, 1997).

Gibbons, D.S. and S. Kasim, *Banking on the Rural Poor* (Penang: University Sains, 1991).

Gibbons, D.S. and J.W. Meehan, 'The Microcredit Summit's Challenge: Working Toward Institutional Financial Self-sufficiency while Maintaining a Commitments to Serving the Poorest Families', *Journal of Microfinance*, 1 (1) (1991).

Gonzalez-Vega, C., 'From Policies to Technologies, to Organizations: The Evolution for the Ohio State University Vision of Rural Financial Markets', *Economic and Sociology Occasional Paper* No. 2062, Ohio State University, Columbus (1993).

Goodhart, C., et al., *Financial Regulation: Why, How and Where Now?* (London: Routledge, 1998).

Goodwin-Groen, R., *The Role of Commercial Bank in Microfinance: Asia-Pacific Region* (Brisbane: Foundation for Development Cooperation, 1998).

Gulli, H., *Microfinance and Poverty: Questioning the Conventional Wisdom* (Washington D.C.: Inter-American Development Bank, 1998).

Hanning, A. and E. Katimbo-Mugwanya, 'How to Regulate and Supervise Microfinance: Key Issues in an International Perspective', *Financial Systems Development Series*, No. 1, November (1999).

Hardy, D.C., P. Holder and V. Prokopenko, 'Microfinance Institutions and Public Policy', *IMF Working Paper*, 02/159, September (2002).

Harper, M., *Small Business in the Third World* (Chichester: John Wiley and Sons, 1984).

Harper, M., *Profit for the Poor: Cases in Microfinance* (London: Intermediate Technology Publications, 1998).

Harper, M. (ed.), *Microfinance. Evolution, Achievements and Challenges* (London: ITDG Publishing, 2003).

Helms, B. and X. Reille, 'Interest Rate Ceilings And Microfinance: The Story So Far', CGAP Occasional Paper, No. 9, September (2004).

Herath, G., 'Rural Credit Market and Institutional Reform in Developing Countries: Potential and Problems', *Savings and Development*, 18 (2) (1994).

Hertz, N., *Un pianeta in debito* (Milan: Ponte alle grazie, 2005).

Hoff, K., A. Braverman and J.E. Stiglitz, *The Economics of Rural Organization: Theory, Practice and Policy* (New York: Oxford University Press, 1993).

Holtmann, M. et al., *Developing Staff Incentive Schemes*. MicroSave, November, (2002).

Hulme, D., 'Can the Grameen Bank be Replicated? Recent Experiments in Malaysia, Malawi and Sri Lanka', *Development Policy Review*, 8 (3) (1990).

Hulme, D., 'Impact Assessment Methodologies for Microfinance: Theory, Experiences and Better Practice', *World Development*, 28 (1), (2000) 79–98.

Hulme, D. and R. Montgomery, 'Co-operatives, Credit and the Poor: Private Interest, Public Choice and Collective Action in Sri Lanka', *Savings and Development*, 18 (3) (1994).

Hulme, D. and P. Mosley, *Finance Against Poverty*, Vols I and II, (London: Routledge, 1996).

Hulme, D. and P. Mosley, 'Finance for the Poor or the Poorest? Financial Innovation, Poverty and Vulnerability', in *Who Needs Credit? Poverty and Finance in Bangladesh* (eds) G.D. Wood and I. Sharif (Dhaka: University Press Limited, 1997).

Inter-American Development Bank, 'The Microfinance Industry: Does it Measure Up?', *Microenterprise Development Review*, August (1999).

Intonti, M., *Valore Economico e Comportamento Etico nelle Imprese Bancarie* (Bari: Cacucci Editore, 2004).

Jackelen, H.R. and E. Rhyne, 'Towards a More Market-oriented Approach to Credit and Savings for the Poor', in M. Harper (ed.), *Microfinance. Evolution, Achievements and Challenges* (London: ITDG Publishing, 2003).

Jansson, T., R. Rosales and G. D. Westley, *Principles and Practices for Regulating and Supervising Microfinance*, Inter-American Development Bank, New York, (2004).

Jenkins, H., 'Commercial Bank Behaviour in Micro and Small Enterprise Finance', *Development Discussion Paper*, No. 741, Harvard Institute for International Development, February (2000).

Johnson, S. et al., 'The Managed ASCA Model: Innovation in Kenya's Microfinance Industry', in M. Harper (ed.), *Microfinance. Evolution, Achievements and Challenges* (London: ITDG Publishing, 2003).

Johnson, S. and B. Rogaly, *Microfinance and Poverty Reduction* (London: Intermediate Technology Publications, 1997).

Khalily, B. and R. Meyer, 'Factors Influencing the Demand for Rural Deposits in Bangladesh: a Test for Functional Form', *Journal of Developing Areas*, 26 (1993).

Khandker, S., B. Khalily and Z. Khan, 'Grameen Bank: Performance and Sustainability', *World Bank Discussion Paper*, No. 206, Washington D.C. (1995).

Khawari, A., 'Microfinance: Does it hold its promises? A Survey of Recent Literature', *Hamburgisches Weltwirtschaftsarchiv Discussion Paper*, No. 276 (2004).

Kimenyi, M.S., R.C. Wieland and J.D. Von Pischke, *Strategic Issues in Microfinance* (Aldershot: Ashgate, 1998).

Lapenu, C. and M. Zeller, 'Distribution, Growth, and Performance of Microfinance Institutions in Africa, Asia, and Latin America: A Recent Inventory', *Savings and Development*, 1 (26) (2002) 87–111.

La Torre, M. 'Microfinanza e Finanza Etica', *Bancaria*, 10 (2005).

La Torre, M. and G. Vento, 'Per una nuova microfinanza: il ruolo delle banche', *Bancaria*, 2 (2005).

Ledgerwood, J., *Microfinance Handbook* (Washington D.C.: World Bank: 2000).

Levitsky, J. (ed.), *Microenterprises in Developing Countries* (London: Intermediate Technology Publications, 1989).

Lovell, C.H., 'Breaking the Cycle of Poverty: The BRAC Strategy' (Connecticut: Kumarian Press, 1992).

Mahajan, V. and B.G. Ramola, 'Financial Services for the Rural Poor and Women in India: Access and Sustainability', *Journal of International Development*, 8 (2) (1996) 211–24.

Matin, I., D. Hulme and S. Rutherford, 'Financial Services for the Poor and the Poorest: Deepening Understanding to Improve Provison', Institute of Development Policy and Management (IDPM), University of Manchester, Finance and Development Working Paper, No. 9 (1999).

McAllister, P. and S. Tenn, *Achieving Financial Sustainability: Six Key Strategies For Microfinance Associations* (Washington D.C.: SEEP Network, 2004).

McVay, M., *Performance Measurement for Business Development Services: A Preliminary Framework*, Microenterprise Best Practices (1999).

Meagher, P., *Microfinance Regulation in Developing Countries: A Comparative Review of Current Practice*, IRIS Center, University of Maryland, mimeo, October (2002).

Meehan, J., 'Tapping the Financial Market for Microfinance: Grameen Foundation USA's Promotion of this Emerging Trend', *Grameen Foundation USA Working Paper Series* (2004).

Meyer, R.L., B. Khalily and J.L. Hushak, 'Bank Branches and Rural Deposits: Evidence from Bangladesh', *Economy and Sociology Occasional Paper*, No. 1462, Ohio State University (1988).

MicroBanking Bulletin, Calmeadow: Toronto and Washington D.C. (1999 and 2003).

Microrate–Inter-American Development Bank, *Performance Indicators for Microfinance Institutions: Technical Guide*, 3rd edn (New York: Inter-American Development Bank, July 2003).

Miracle, M., S.D. Miracle and L. Cohen, 'Informal Savings Mobilization in Africa', *Economic Development and Cultural Change*, 28 (4) (1980) 701–21.

Morduch, J., 'The Microfinance Schism', *World Development*, 28 (4) (1998) 617–29.

Mosley, P., 'Optimal Incentives to Repay in Institutions Lending to Low Income Groups: an Indonesian Case Study', *Savings and Development*, 19 (3) (1995).

Morduch, J., 'The Microfinance Promise', *Journal of Economic Literature*, 37 (4) (1999) 1569–614.

Natilson, N. and T.A. Bruett, *Financial Performance Monitoring: A Guide for Board Members of Microfinance Institutions*, Microenterprise Best Practices, September (2001).

Navajas, S. et al., 'Microfinance and the Poorest of the Poor: Theory and Evidence from Bolivia', *World Development*, 28 (2000).

Nayar, C.P.S., 'Can Traditional Financial Technologies Co-exist with Modern Technologies? The Indian Experience', *Savings and Development*, 10 (1) (1986).

Nowak, M., *Non si presta solo ai ricchi. La rivoluzione del microcredito* (Turin: Gli struzzi Einaudi, 2005).

Otero, M., 'Bringing Development Bank into Microfinance', *Journal of Microfinance*, 1 (1) (1999).

Otero, M. and E. Rhyne (eds), *The New World of Microenterprise Finance: Building Healthy Financial Institutions for the Poor* (Hartford: Kumarian Press, 1994).

Paxton, J., *A Worldwide Inventory of Microfinance Institutions*, (Washington D.C.: World Bank, 1996).

Pesic, V., 'Implementazione e auditing del sistema dei controlli interni in banca: una risposta alla problematica del governo della complessità aziendale', *Quaderni del Dottorato di Ricerca in Gestione Bancaria e Finanziaria*, No. 2 (Rome: Edizioni Kappa, 2005).

Quinones, B.R. Jr., 'Financial Instruments for Small Enterprises', *Asia Pacific Rural Finance*, Bangkok, Thailand (1991).

Quinones, B.R. Jr. and E. Kropp, *Financial Intermediation System in Support of the People's Economy* (Bangkok: Apraca, 1992).

Remenyi, J., 'Is There a "State of the Art" in Microfinance?', in J. Remenyi and B. Quinones Jr. (eds), *Microfinance and Poverty Alleviation. Case Studies from Asia and the Pacific* (New York: Pinter, 2000).

Remenyi, J. and Quinones B. Jr. (eds), *Microfinance and Poverty Alleviation. Case Studies from Asia and the Pacific* (New York: Pinter, 2000).

Rhyne, E., 'The Yin and Yang of Microfinance: Reaching the poor and sustainability', in *MicroBanking Bulletin*, University of Colorado, July (1997).

Robinson, M.S., *Local Politics: The Law of the Fishes* (New Delhi: Oxford University Press, 1988).

Robinson, M.S., 'Financial Intermediation at the Local Level: Lessons from Indonesia', Part One, Harvard Institute for International Development, *Discussion Paper*, No. 434, Cambridge, MA (1992).

Robinson, M.S., 'Savings Mobilization and Microenterprise Finance: The Indonesian Experience', in M. Otero and E. Rhyne (eds), *The New World of Microenterprise Finance: Building Healthy Financial Institutions for the Poor* (West Hartford: Kumarian Press, 1994a).

Robinson, M.S., 'Financial Intermediation at the Local Level: Lessons from Indonesia, Part Two: The Theoretical Perspective', Harvard Institute for International Development, *Discussion Paper*, No. 482, Cambridge, MA (1994b).

Robinson, M.S., 'Introducing Savings Mobilization in Microfinance Programs: When and How?', Microfinance Network (Cavite, Philippines, November, 1995a).

Robinson, M.S., 'The Paradigm Shift in Microfinance: A Perspective from HID', Harvard Institute for International Development, *Discussion Paper*, No. 510, Cambridge, MA (1995b).

Robinson, M.S., 'Answering Some Key Questions on Finance and Poverty, in The New World of Microfinance, Conference Proceedings', *Coalition for Microfinance Standards*, Philippines (1997).

Robinson, M.S., 'Microfinance: the Paradigm Shift from Credit Delivery to Sustainable Financial Intermediation', in M.S. Kimenyi, R.C. Wieland and J.D. Von Pischke, *Strategic Issues in Microfinance* (Aldershot: Ashgate, 1998).

Robinson, M.S., *The Microfinance Revolution: Sustainable Finance for the Poor*, Volume 1 (Washington D.C.: World Bank, 2001).

Robinson, M.S., *The Microfinance Revolution: Lessons from Indonesia*, Volume 2 (Washington D.C.: World Bank, 2002).

Rosenberg, R. et al., *Disclosure Guidelines for Financial Reporting by Microfinancial Institutions*, CGAP/World Bank Group, July (2003).

Rutherford, S., *ASA: The Biography of an NGO*, Association of Social Advancement, Dhaka (1995).

Rutherford, S., *A Critical Typology of Financial Services for the Poor*, ActionAid, London (1996).

Rutherford, S., 'The Savings of the Poor: Improving Financial Services in Bangladesh', *Journal of International Development*, 10 (1) (1998) 1–15.

Rutherford, S., *The Poor and their Money* (New Delhi: Oxford University Press, 2000).

Rutherford, S., 'Raising the Curtain on the Microfinancial Credit Era', in M. Harper (ed.), *Microfinance. Evolution, Achievements and Challenges* (London: ITDG Publishing, 2003).

Saita, F., *Il risk management in banca* (Milan: Egea, 2000).

Saltzman, S.B. and D. Salinger, 'The ACCION CAMEL', Microenterprise Best Practices Project Technical Note, September 1998.

Santoboni, F., 'L'evoluzione della regolamentazione e dei controlli nel Sistema finanziario secondo l'approccio organizzativo sistemico complesso', *Quaderni del Dottorato di Ricerca in Gestione Bancaria e Finanziaria*, 2 (Rome: Edizioni Kappa, 2005).

Schreiner, M., *Thinking About the Performance and Sustainability of Microfinance Organizations*, Microfinance, August (1996) Available at <www.microfinance.com>.

Schreiner, M., *A Framework for the Analysis of Performance and Sustainability*, PHD Dissertation, Ohio University (1997a).

Schreiner, H. (ed.), *Microfinance for the Poor?* (Paris: OECD, 1997b).

Schreiner, M., *Aspects of Outreach: A Framework for the Discussion of the Social Benefits of Microfinance* (St Louis: Microfinance, 1999).

Schreiner, M., 'Ways Donors Can Help the Evolution of Sustainable Microfinance Organizations', *Savings and Development*, 24 (4) (2000) 423–37.

Schreiner, M., 'Scoring: the Next Breakthrough in Microcredit?', Consultative Group to Assist the Poorest, *Occasional Paper*, No. 7, January (2003).

Schreiner, M. and J. Leon, *Microfinance for Microenterprise: a Source Book for Donors*, Microfinance Risk Management, November (2001).

Schreiner, M. et al., 'Microcredit and the Poorest of the Poor: Theory and Evidence from Bolivia', *World Development*, 28 (1) (2000) 333–46.

Schrieder, G. and F. Heidhues, 'Reaching the Poor Through Financial Innovations', *Quarterly Journal of International Agriculture*, 34 (2) (1995) 132–48.

Seibel, H.D., *Financial Systems Development and Microfinance*, Deutsche Gesellschaft fur Technische Zusammenarbeit, Rossdorf, Eschborn (1996).

Shaw, E.S., *Financial Deepening in Economic Development* (New York: Oxford University Press, 1973).

Simanowitz, A. and K. Powlak, *Social Performance Management in Microfinance: Guidelines* (Institute of Development Studies, 2005).

Simons, R., *Performance Measurement and Control Systems for Implementing Strategy*, Prentice Hall (2000).

Sironi, A., *Rischio e valore nelle banche* (Milan: Egea, 2005).

Staschen S., *Regulation and Supervision of Microfinance Institutions: State of Knowledge*, Deutsche Gesellschaft für Technische Zusammenarbeit (GTZ) GmbH, mimeo, August (1999).

Staschen, S., *Regulatory Requirements for Microfinance*, Deutsche Gesellschaft für Technische Zusammenarbeit (GTZ) GmbH, mimeo (2003).

Stiglitz, J., Peer Monitoring and Credit Markets, *World Bank Economic Review*, 4 (3) (1990) 351–66.

The SEEP Network/Calmeadow, *Financial Ratio Analysis of Microfinance Institutions* (1995).

Tulchin, D., 'Positioning Microfinance Institutions for the Capital Markets', *Social Enterprise Associates Working Paper*, No. 5 (2004).

Tutino, F., G. Bastianini, M. Parancandolo, *La performance delle banche* (Rome: Bancaria Editrice, 2005).

Van Greuning, H., J. Gallardo and B. Randhawa, *A Framework for Regulating Microfinance Institutions*, December (Washington D.C.: World Bank, 1998).

Varian, H., 'Monitoring Agents with other Agents', *Journal of Institutional and Theoretical Economics*, 146 (1990).

Vento, G.A., 'New Challenges in Microfinance: the Importance of Regulation', *Centro de Estudios de la Estructura Economica*, University of Buenos Aires, 2004.

Vento, G.A., 'Microfinance for cooperation: sustainability, performance and legal framework', *Politica Internazionale*, 1–2/3 (2005).

Versluysen, E., *Defying the Odds: Banking for the Poor* (West Hartford: Kumarian Press, 1999).

Viganò, L. (eds), *Microfinanza in Europa* (Milan: Giuffré Editore, 2004).

Vincenzini, M. and P. Porretta, *Le 'immagini' della creazione del valore di impresa ... e aneddoti bancari* (Padua: Cedam, 2004).

Vogel, R.C., 'Savings Mobilization: The Forgotten Half of Rural Finance', in D.W. Adams, D.H. Graham and J.D. Von Pischke, *Undermining Rural Development with Cheap Credit* (Boulder: Westview Press, 1984).

Von Pischke, J.D., *Finance at the Frontier: Debt Capacity and the Role of Credit in the Private Economy* (Washington D.C.: World Bank, 1991).

Von Pischke, J.D., 'Measuring the Trade-Off Between Outreach and Sustainability of Microenterprise', *Journal of International Development*, 8 (2) (1996).

Von Pischke, J.D., D.W. Adams and G. Donald (eds), *Rural Financial Markets in Developing Countries: Their Use and Abuse* (Baltimore: Johns Hopkins University Press, 1983).

Von Stauffenberg, D., 'Definitions of Selected Financial terms, Ratios and Adjustments for Microfinance', *Microbanking Bulletin*, November (2002).

Wahid, A. (ed.), *The Grameen Bank: Poverty Relief in Bangladesh* (Boulder: Westview, 1993).

Woller, G. and M. Schreiner, *Poverty Lending, Financial Self-Sufficiency, and the Six Aspects of Outreach* (Utah: Marriot School, Brigham Young University, 2002).

Woolcock, M.J.V., 'Learning from Failures in Microfinance: What Unsuccessful Cases Tell Us How Group Based Programs Work', *American Journal of Economics and Sociology*, 58 (1) (1999).

World Bank, 'A Review of Bank Lending for Agricultural Credit and Rural Finances, 1948–1992', *Operations Evaluations Department Report*, No. 12143, Washington, D.C. (1993).

World Bank, 'World Bank Lending for Small Enterprises, 1989–1993', *World Bank Technical Paper*, No. 311, Washington, D.C. (1996a).

World Bank, *Poverty Reduction and the World Bank: Progress and Challenges in the 1990s* (Washington D.C.: World Bank, 1996b).

World Bank, *From Plan to Market. World Development Report 1996* (Washington D.C.: World Bank, 1996c).

Wright, G.A.N., 'The Impact of Microfinance Services: Increasing Income or Reducing Poverty?', *Small Enterprise Development*, 10 (1) London (1999).

Wright, G.A.N., *Microfinance Systems. Designing Quality Financial Services for the Poor* (London and New York: Zed Books Ltd, 2000).

Wright, G.A.N. et al., *Looking Before You Leap: Key Questions That Should Precede Starting New Development Products*, MicroSave–Africa Essay (2001).

Yaron, J., 'Assessing Development Finance Institutions. A Public Interest Analysis', *Policy Research Working Paper*, No. 174 (Washington D.C.: World Bank, 1992).

Yaron, J., 'What Makes Rural Finance Institutions Successful?', *World Bank Research Observer*, 9 (9) (1994) 49–70.

Yaron, J., M.P. Benjamin and G.L. Piprek, *Rural Finance: Issues, Design, and Best Practices* (Washington D.C.: World Bank, 1997).

Young, R., L. Mitten and C. Falgon, *Legal Frameworks and Performance Standards for Microfinance: A Desk Study* (USAID, 2000).

Yunus, M., *The Grameen Bank: Experiences and Reflections* (Dhaka: Grameen Bank, 1991).

Yunus, M., *Banker to the Poor: The Autobiography of Muhammad Yunus, Founder of the Grameen Bank* (New York: Oxford University Press, 2001).

Zeller, M. and R.L. Meyer (eds), *The Triangle of Microfinance. Financial Sustainability, Outreach, and Impact* (Baltimore: Johns Hopkins University Press, 2002).

Useful Web Sites

www.accion.org
www.acdi-cida.gc.ca/microcredit
www.adb.org
www.alternative-finance.org.uk
www.bancaetica.com
www.bancosol.org.bo
www.bilanciosociale.it
www.bwtp.org
www.calmeadow.com
www.cgap.org
www.choros.it
www.csreurope.org
www.developmentgap.org
www.devinit.org
www.etimos.it
www.european-microfinance.org
www.gdrc.org
www.grameen.org
www.icsitalia.org
www.ifard.org
www.ilo.org
www.imf.org
www.improntaetica.org
www.lavoroetico.it
www.mag6.it
www.mfc.org.pl
www.microcreditsummit.org
www.microfinancegateway.org
www.microfinancement.cirad.fr
www.microfinanza.com
www.microrate.com
www.microsave.org
www.microsave-africa.com
www.mip.org
www.mixmarket.org
www.myrada.org
www.noprofit.org
www.oneworld.org
www.ong.it

www.orsadata.it
www.planetfinance.org
www.postconflictmicrofinance.org
www.ratingfund.org
www.seepnetwork.org
www.swwb.org
www.uncdf.org
www.undp.org
www.unimondo.org
www.woccu.org
www.worldbank.org
www.yearofmicrocredit.org

Index